INSTANT
CREDIT
REPAIR

SIMPLE, FAST &
EASY FORMS
FOR GREAT CREDIT

by

James J. Shapiro, J.D., L.L.M.

DISCLAIMER AND LIMITED WARRANTY

This publication is designed to provide general information about why we need more lawyers and more lawsuits. No author or lawyer should give professional advice about a specific problem or question unless he or she knows all of the facts and circumstances surrounding the particular case and the individual client.

Buying or reading this book does not make you a client of the author. You become a client by making an agreement for representation with a particular lawyer. Such agreements are generally put in writing, in the form of a retainer statement that the lawyer would ask you to sign.

The laws in every state vary. Every problem or case has different facts and circumstances. The author, publisher, distributor and retailer specifically disclaim any personal liability, loss, or risk incurred as a consequence of the use, either directly or indirectly, as of result of any information in this book. The author and publisher are not engaged in rendering legal, accounting, insurance, or other professional services by publishing this book. If legal advice or other expert assistance is required, the services of a competent professional person should be sought.

100% MONEY BACK GUARANTEE

You have nothing to lose and everything to gain. You can try and test our book and forms at your own risk, with a complete money back satisfaction guarantee.

YES!! Just try the simple-to-use forms included in our "Instant Credit Repair" book. If after 3 months you have not improved your credit and have followed our steps, we will give you back all of your money. That's right – just mail out our forms. If you, for any reason, are not happy with your results, we will give you a 100% refund!!!

In order to request a refund, please mail your copy of our book and a copy of your sales slip to: Boca Press LLC, 700 First Federal Plaza, Rochester, NY 14614. Within 90 days, we will issue you a refund for the amount of the purchase price.

IN MEMORY OF MY FATHER
DEDICATION TO SIDNEY S. SHAPIRO

To a very special person, my best friend, mentor, constant supporter, and great understanding dad.

My dad was always around to talk with me, for my first 46 years. We would talk about family, golf, clients, helping people, and our loud television ads. He was a calm, gentle man that just wanted to help others.

On Halloween, October 31, 2004, my dad passed away in my home, from cancer.

My father practiced law for more than 50 years, and helped thousands of people. Lawyers, judges, and clients praised his compassionate heart. I was lucky to have known him and to be his son. I will miss him every day.

What I have learned most from my father is that the more you help others, and try to do good for your fellow man, the better all of our lives will be. I strive to practice this daily in honor of my father.

-- Jim Shapiro

ABOUT THE AUTHOR

Jim "The Hammer" Shapiro is a tough, smart, aggressive lawyer who has made a lifetime commitment to helping victims win cash awards. By telling secrets the insurance companies hope you will never know, "The Hammer" has helped thousands of people.

"The Hammer" cares about people and he proves it! He completed a donation of $823,000.00 for a new YMCA. "The Hammer" has donated thousands of books to school children who could not afford books. "The Hammer" has also donated tens of thousands to help build schools for children. Shapiro has donated thousands more to help children read.

"The Hammer" is a recognized authority on injury law. He is the author of five books with more than 40,000 books in print! He is the author of "Victims Rights to Maximum Cash", "Sue the Bastards", "Million Dollar Lungs", "Injury Victims Rights to Maximum Cash", and "Get Back All Your Lost Investments!"

"The Hammer" has been seen and heard by millions on:

"The Phil Donahue Show"

CNBC

Time Magazine

Over 500 ABC News Stations

Local Radio and TV stations

WORK, WROC, WSTM, WKTV, WNBC

Rochester Times Union

Radio Free Europe

USA Today

Syracuse Newspapers

New York Times

Miami Herald

Sun Sentinel

Boca Raton News

Leeza

Jim "The Hammer" Shapiro is the founder of three law firms. He graduated from Boston University Law School's Masters Program, is a member of the New York and Florida Bar, and the Plaintiff's Securities Lawyers Group. "The Hammer" had offices in Broward County, Florida, as well as Rochester, Syracuse, and Buffalo, New York.

Jim "The Hammer" Shapiro helped more than 5,000 people to collect more than 100 Million Dollars.

"The Hammer" reached the public with TV ads stating, "I am the meanest, nastiest SOB in town." All the other lawyers hated "The Hammer" for his success. He did not care about the hate. He cared for the injured victim and was the first in the country to LOWER LEGAL FEES FOR INJURY VICTIMS.

Shapiro was the first to run TV and newspaper ads stating "LEGAL FEES SLASHED BY 40%" and "WHY PAY 33%, ONLY PAY 19.9%" for injury claims settled without starting a lawsuit.

Shapiro sold all 3 law firms and is now writing books to help the "less than average Joe."

A major goal of Shapiro is to educate injury victims about their rights to HUGE CASH AWARDS and their rights to pay lawyers 40% less in legal fees. This means more money to injury victims.

Jim "The Hammer" can be reached at 1-800-285-9211.

TABLE OF CONTENTS

(To dispute debts, you must first have a list of all debts owed. So, get a copy of your credit report to look for

forgotten or unknown debts.)

CHAPTER 1

FIX YOUR CREDIT

Do you know that insurance companies often charge people with bad credit higher car and homeowner insurance rates?

Do you know that credit card companies deny you credit or give you small credit limits because of your bad credit report?

Do you know that banks and finance companies charge more than double the interest charges daily if you have bad credit?

Do you know that to lease a car at a great rate, you must have great credit?

FORTUNATELY, THERE IS AN ANSWER

This book includes the simple, fast & easy forms for great credit.

YOU CAN FIX YOUR CREDIT. YOU CAN PAY LESS FOR AUTO AND HOME INSURANCE. YOU CAN PAY FAR LESS FOR AUTO LOANS. YOU CAN HAVE GOOD CREDIT.

You will learn little known laws that drive creditors crazy. Nothing in the book is unethical. Nothing in the book is wrong. It has taken years of research and real use of these forms to prepare this simple, effective report and forms book.

So simple that anyone can use these forms to get great credit.

CREATED BY A LAWYER

YES!!! "Clean Credit" was prepared and edited by a lawyer, James J. Shapiro, J.D., L.L.M. Why is this important? Because "Clean Credit" is all about the legal and simple ways to get great credit, without paying an agency to do this for you. Disputing your past credit mistakes is a matter for experts. You have thousands of dollars at stake, and you need an honest and fast way to get great credit.

ITS SO EASY TO USE

You do not need legal training. There is nothing to memorize. You do not need a high school diploma. You do need to know what to mail, and how to mail it. "Clean Credit,"

tells you in simple language, and with simple to use forms, how

to have great credit.

IT IS LEGAL TO USE OUR FORMS
EVEN IF YOU OWE THE MONEY!!!

That's right. Even if you owe money, you have a legal

right to send out the forms included in "Clean Credit." Federal

laws require the creditor to reply promptly with certain

information that you will request. If you do not receive a

timely response, the credit bureau must promptly clean your

credit! If the creditor responds promptly, but does not include

all the required information, again, the credit bureau must

promptly clean your credit!!! This little known information,

and so much more are included in this book.

CHAPTER 2

THE BIG PICTURE
(READ THIS FIRST)

You owe money, have not paid, or have paid late. You can fix your credit report. Just follow these easy steps.

1) Obtain your credit reports from all 3 credit bureaus to be sure you have all the debts and late payments, judgments, bad public records, collections, and other marks on your credit.

2) Send the verification letters included in this book. If the credit bureau does not promptly and properly verify your debts per the Fair Credit Reporting Act and Fair Debt Collection Practices Act, you can often

have the bad remarks removed. Yes, bad credit, judgments, public records, and all bad credit remarks can be removed, even if you paid late or owe the money.

3) In the event the bad credit marks are properly verified, many people have done the following with great results:

    I.   Wait 45 days and ask for verification again. Often, the credit bureaus get too busy to respond in time or with the proper information. Some report that the first week in December is a great time to request validation. You should include the following response:

State that the credit-reporting agency must delete the negative items from your credit report.

If they determine that your disputes are frivolous or irrelevant, they must provide the reasons for their determination per Section 611(a)(3)(C) within 5 days, and must provide a description of their procedures used to determine the accuracy and completeness of the information, along with any contact information per Section 611(a)(6)(B)(iii) of the Fair Credit Reporting Act.

End by stating that their failure to either delete the information or provide the requested information, will be considered willful noncompliance to the Fair Credit Reporting Act and damages will be pursued against them, as allowed under Section 616(a)(1)(A).

Be sure to send your correspondence via certified mail, return receipt requested. When they fail to respond, consider filing a small claims lawsuit.

II.   Review the responses to your verification letters and find misstatements about your debt, name or bad credit history. Prepare small claims lawsuit papers (and do not file them with any court) stating that the credit bureau did not properly verify your debts. A good argument is that since the credit bureaus could not provide credible evidence of a debt existing that the credit bureaus cannot legally maintain the bad credit remark on the credit report.

You do not need to sue the credit bureaus based on the accounts being valid. You can sue the credit bureaus for alleged violations of the Fair Credit Reporting Act. For example, not properly verifying debts as valid within the 30 days. Include copies of all of your previous dispute letters.

Consider starting your lawsuit for not providing enough proof and violation by the credit-reporting agency for maintaining an unverifiable negative trade line. Also, you may allege that the credit bureaus do not have adequate controls in place to guarantee that only accurate data is reflected on the reports they provide as shown in the 1997 Trans Union lawsuit.

Always include with your lawsuit a copy of the 1997 Trans Union lawsuit. Deliver a copy of the Trans Union lawsuit and your small claims lawsuit to the President of each credit bureau that you desire to fix your credit.

Be sure to use a cover letter detailing the deletions you desire.

Most credit bureaus desire to avoid the huge costs of hiring a lawyer to defend themselves.

Think about it. The credit bureaus maintain 180 million credit reports. Can they afford to defend your lawsuit?

III.   If all else fails, file your lawsuit papers with the small claims court. Serve a copy on the credit bureau at Trans Union, Experian, and Equifax. Prior to court, the credit bureau can offer to delete your remarks. If you must go to court, be honest. For example, if true, tell the Judge that you are not sure you owe the debt, as you did not receive the required information to verify the debt.

IV.   If you are so unlucky that the above small claims court does not work, your best options are to 1) repeat steps I, II, and III, above, or 2) make a plan to repay part of the debt over the next 12 months in exchange for removal of the bad mark on your credit, or 3) file for bankruptcy. Yes, after bankruptcy you will have no more debts and you will probably be able to get credit right away. It is not unusual to have very good credit just 18 months after bankruptcy.

The reason most of these ideas work is because big credit bureaus have a hard time finding exact records as required by law. It is not easy for a credit bureau to provide all of these items: a statement, signed copy of your opening of the account, and a signed sales receipt.

Most credit bureaus do not want to fight a long battle, and the Fair Credit Reporting Act provides for $1,000.00 in penalties per violation by a credit bureau. Additionally, you may be entitled to punitive damages. Lawyers charge the credit bureaus a fortune to defend any small claims case you bring. In the long run, a lawsuit brought about by you can cost the credit bureau more money that it is worth for them to fight your requests.

CHAPTER 3

GET YOUR CREDIT REPORTS

You want great credit. The first step is to get your credit reports from each of the three main reporting agencies. We recommend that you obtain each one, as your creditors may not report your information to the same agency. Know what credit information is out there.

You are entitled to a free credit report if you have just been denied credit based on the report. Also, you may be able to obtain one free copy of your credit report each year, depending on your situation. If you must purchase your credit report, you can contact each of the three agencies and purchase the report for a fee, generally less than $10.00 per report. You may also wish to request your credit score.

Here are the details: if you have been denied credit for any reason, you are entitled to receive a copy of the credit report from the agency that provided the report to your creditor, as long as you request the report within 60 days. Creditors are required to notify you of this right, in writing, at the time of the written denial.

The 3 major credit reporting agencies are:

Equifax 1-800-685-1111 www.equifax.com

Experian 1-888-397-3742 www.experian.com

Trans Union 1-800-916-8800 www.transunion.com

At this time, you may also choose to sign up for a service that helps you to monitor your credit report. They generally charge an annual fee and will notify you every time any new information is reported on your credit. We will review this later in the book.

Once you have requested your report, it should arrive within 10 business days, or you can often get the report instantly online.

CHAPTER 3 FORM: FREE REQUEST FOR CREDIT REPORT BASED ON ANY DENIAL OF CREDIT

You are often entitled to a free credit report.
Use this form letter to get a free report.

Dear Credit Reporting Agency:

I have been denied credit within the last 60 days based on a credit report you provided.

Please send me a FREE copy of my credit report to my address below.

My name is _____
My address is_____
My social security number is _____
My date of birth is _____
Thank you.

Very truly yours,

(Sign your name here)

CHAPTER 4

MAKE A LIST OF ALL YOUR BAD CREDIT REMARKS AND DEBTS OWED

You can dispute any bad credit information on your report. Consider disputing all of these items for each report:

1. Negative public records;

2. Accounts in collection;

3. Accounts past due;

4. Charge offs;

5. Credit inquiries hurt your credit score;

6. Wrong address, occupation, date of birth, or social security number;

7. Serious delinquency;

8. Past due payments due on any account.

To be certain you have all the negative information, call anyone you applied for credit with. They can tell you what is wrong with your report.

CHAPTER 4 FORM:
LIST OF ALL BAD CREDIT REMARKS
ON THE CREDIT REPORT

Item	Credit Bureau	Specify Details of Remarks Public Records, Late Payments, & Collections, etc.
1.		
2.		
3.		
4.		
5.		
6.		
7.		
8.		
9.		
10.		
11.		

CHAPTER 5

SIMPLE FORM LETTERS TO DISPUTE DEBTS AND TO FOLLOW-UP ON INITIAL DISPUTE

To dispute any bad credit on your report, send a letter, certified mail, and include all items that are not accurate on your credit report, using the following letter as a guide.

It has been reported on Internet chat rooms that people who dispute all negative items can get them all removed. Of course, our advice is to only include the items you desire to dispute as inaccurate. We do not recommend you to dispute factual listings. However, you still have the right to request that any negative information be removed from your credit report that is not properly verified. So, word your dispute letter carefully to ask for verification without disputing any truthful statements on your report.

IMPORTANT ITEM:

YOU HAVE THE RIGHT TO REQUEST THAT EACH AND EVERY NEGATIVE ITEM BE VERIFIED.

FOLLOWING YOUR REQUEST FOR VERIFICATION, YOU HAVE THE RIGHT TO REQUEST THAT ANY NEGATIVE INFORMATION BE REMOVED FROM YOUR CREDIT REPORT, IF IT IS NOT PROMPTLY VERIFIED.

CHAPTER 5 FORM:

DISPUTE LETTER - INITIAL LETTER TO CREDIT BUREAU

Dear Credit Bureau:

Via Certified Mail
Return Receipt Requested

RE: Full Name
        Social Security Number
        Date of Birth

I am disputing (insert item in question) on my credit report.

State the reason you are disputing the item.

I request you to investigate this, and if you do not verify it, remove this information from my credit file.

If this entry is removed, I request notification by you to me confirming this has happened. My request is made according to 611(d) of the Fair Credit Reporting Act.

Best regards.

Very truly yours,

(Insert your signature here)

CHAPTER 5 FORM:

VALIDATION LETTER – ALTERNATE INITIAL LETTER TO CREDIT BUREAU

Dear Credit Bureau:

> Via Certified Mail
> Return Receipt Requested

RE: Full Name
       Social Security Number
       Date of Birth

I am requesting validation and proof of: (insert item in question) on my credit report.

I request you to investigate this, and if you do not verify it, remove this information from my credit file.

If this entry is removed, I request notification by you to me confirming this has happened. My request is made according to 611(d) of the Fair Credit Reporting Act.

Best regards.

Very truly yours,

(Insert your signature here)

CHAPTER 5 FORM:

DISPUTE LETTER #2 (MAIL THIS AFTER 30 DAYS, OR CONSIDER USING DISPUTE LETTER #3)

Dear Credit Bureau: Via Certified Mail
                                       Return Receipt Requested

    RE: Full Name
             Social Security Number
             Date of Birth

This letter is formal notice that you have failed to respond to my dispute *(or validation)* letter of 30 days ago dated (insert date of first letter.) I sent this letter to you via Registered Mail and have enclosed a copy of my proof of your receipt thereof.

As you are aware, you have 30 days from your receipt to respond. Failure to follow and comply with the Fair Credit Reporting Act 15 U.S.C. 1681i(5)(A) is a serious allegation that may be investigated by the FTC. Obviously, I am keeping detailed records of all my correspondence with you.

I am including another copy of my original request. Please remove and delete these items today, and verify your deletion by sending me a copy of my corrected report.

The following needs to be verified and deleted from my credit report as soon as possible: _____.

Very truly yours,
(Insert your signature here)

CHAPTER 5 FORM:

DISPUTE LETTER #3 (CONSIDER THIS FORM LETTER AS FOLLOW-UP TO 1ST LETTER, IF YOU NEED TO)

Dear Credit Card X and Reporting Credit Bureau,

> Via Certified Mail
> Return Receipt Requested

RE: DEMAND TO DELETE ITEMS
       NOT VERIFIED BY YOU

I requested you to fix my credit information, but you have refused, and or did not respond within 30 days. Copies are enclosed of my previous request.

I am well aware that many credit companies fail to credit accounts timely, as required by the Fair Credit Reporting laws, and fail to send out proper and prompt bills.

I am enclosing a copy of the cover page of a recent lawsuit against a credit company showing some of the abuses in your industry.

I am <u>warning</u> you that I will have no choice but to consider legal action if you do not fix my credit report TODAY and remove the unverified (inaccurate) data about my payments, public records, or collections *(include all that are pertinent.)*

I am informing you that I desire to *(refinance, get a credit card, get an auto loan)* in the next 30 days. Your refusal to fix my report will result in a lawsuit asking you to reimburse me for any losses I have including: *(insert if applicable)*

1. Defamation of character;
2. Enablement of identity fraud;
3. Loss of any business opportunities & profits;
4. Any actual damages I sustain by your failure to delete these items; and
5. Costs of the court action, plus attorneys' fees.

I look forward to receiving my corrected credit report.

Best regards,

(Insert your signature, name and Social security number.)

CHAPTER 5 FORM:

DISPUTE LETTER #4
TO INDIVIDUAL DEBT COLLECTORS

Dear Debt Collector,

Via Certified Mail
Return Receipt Requested

RE: Acct. #:
          Customer #:
          Amount:

This letter is being sent to you in response to your attached letter. This is not a refusal to pay, but a notice that your claim is disputed.

This is a request for validation made pursuant to the Fair Debt Collection Practices Act. Please complete the attached form and follow its instructions. Your claim will be processed as soon as it is received, if completed in full with all the requested information.

Please be advised that I am not requesting a "verification" that you have my mailing address. I am requesting a "validation," that is, competent evidence that I have some contractual obligation to pay you.

Please also be aware that if any negative mark is found on my credit reports from your company or any company that represents you, or that you represent, this will result in my filing of an immediate lawsuit against you and your client for:

1) Violation of the Fair Credit Reporting Act;
2) Violation of the Fair Debt Practices Act;
3) Defamation of character;
4) Negligent enablement of identity fraud.

Pending the outcome of my investigation you are instructed to take no action that could be detrimental to any of my credit reports.

Also, if you request payment for a debt you cannot document as due, your name will be forwarded to Federal investigators for mail fraud.

Best Regards,

(Insert your signature, name, and address here)

Please provide the following information to "validate" your obligation. I formally request you to provide the following:

1. Please evidence your authorization under 15 USC 1692(e) and 15 USC 1692(f) in this alleged matter.
2. Please evidence your authorization to do business in this state.

3. What is your authorization of law for your collection of this alleged debt?
4. What is your authorization of law for your collection of information?
5. Please evidence proof of the alleged debt, including specifically the alleged contract or other instruments bearing my signature.

Within 30 days of your receipt of this document, I request that you forward to me copies of all signed contracts evidencing my obligation in regard to the origination of the alleged debt. Along with this, please return the attached disclosure request form. This request form is for "validation" pursuant to the Fair Credit Debt Collection Practices Act.

CREDIT DISCLOSURE STATEMENT

Name and address of debt collector:

_____

Name and address of alleged debtor:

_____

Account number: _____

What are the terms of assignment for this account and attach copies of proof thereof:_____

Has any insurance claim been made by any creditor regarding this account by any creditor or assignee: yes/no

Details:_____

Please list the particular products or services sold by the creditor of the alleged debtor and the dollar amount of each:

_____

Upon failure to provide all requested information to validate this collection action, collector agrees to waive all claims against the alleged debtor named herein.

_____

Authorized signature for collector and date:

_____

Print the name here:_____

Please return this form completed in full and attach all assignment or other transfer agreements that would establish your right to collect this debt. Your claim cannot be considered unless all the information is provided as requested. This information request is pursuant to the Fair Debt Collection Practices Act. If you do not respond as required by this law, your claim will not be considered and you may be liable for damages for continued collection efforts.

Return all documentation and completed forms to:

(Insert your name and address here)

CHAPTER 6

"THE BIG LAWSUIT AGAINST TRANS UNION CORPORATION"

(THIS CHAPTER IS FOR USE WITH STEP 4 & STEP 5)

The most important legal case ever for individuals with bad credit was argued on April 17, 1997.

The case was argued in the United States Court of Appeals for the Third Circuit. The lawsuit was against the credit-reporting agency "Trans Union Corporation." The information you need on this case (No. 95-1553) is included at the end of this chapter.

The lawsuit made clear to all credit reporting agencies that they must "conduct a reasonable reinvestigation of information on a consumer's credit report alleged by the consumer to be inaccurate."

Credit bureaus maintain information on more than 180 million individuals. Most of the staff or investigators are low paid employees who do not have the time or ability to "conduct a reasonable reinvestigation."

Further, a lawsuit by a consumer against a credit-reporting agency would cost the agency thousands of dollars to defend.

The reality is that it is easier for the credit bureau to erase your bad credit than to spend thousands to prove you owe money or did not pay on time.

Remember to use a copy of this case no. 95-1553 against Trans Union Corporation if you need to use Step 3 or Step 4 of the introduction. That is, Step 3 to include a copy of the case with your letter to the credit bureau headquarters c/o the President, warning them that they did not follow the Fair Credit Reporting Act. For Step 4, include a copy of the case with your small claims court action.

The credit bureau will know you mean business and know the law when you include a copy of the case.

Filed June 9, 1997

UNITED STATES COURT OF APPEALS
FOR THE THIRD CIRCUIT

No. 96-1553

JENNIFER CUSHMAN,
    Appellant
v.

TRANS UNION CORPORATION

On Appeal from the United States District Court
for the Eastern District of Pennsylvania
(D.C. No. 95-cv-01743)

Argued April 17, 1997

BEFORE: SCIRICA, COWEN and NYGAARD Circuit Judges

(Filed June 9, 1997)

    Scott D. Godshall, Esq.
    Eric J. Rothschild, Esq. (argued)
    Pepper, Hamilton & Scheetz
    18th & Arch Streets
    3000 Two Logan Square
    Philadelphia, PA 19103-2799

    Counsel for Appellant

Mark E. Kogan, Esq. (argued)
Marion, Satzberg, Trichon & Kogan
1735 Market Street
3000 Mellon Bank Building
Philadelphia, PA 19103

Counsel for Appellee

OPINION OF THE COURT

COWEN, Circuit Judge.

This appeal concerns, among other issues, the extent of a consumer reporting agency's obligation, pursuant to Section 611(a) of the Fair Credit Reporting Act ("FCRA"), 15 U.S.C. 1681i(a) (1982), to conduct a reasonable reinvestigation of information on a consumer's credit report alleged by the consumer to be inaccurate. We hold that the district court erred to the extent that it concluded as a matter of law that defendant Trans Union Corporation ("TUC") fulfilled its obligation under 1681i(a). Therefore, we will reverse and remand the district court's grant of judgment as a matter of law on plaintiff-appellant Jennifer Cushman's claim for negligent noncompliance with that section.

We also hold that Cushman has produced sufficient evidence from which a reasonable jury could find that she has proved the publication element of her defamation claim and her claims pursuant to the Vermont Fair Credit Reporting Act ("VFCRA"), VT. STAT. ANN. tit. 9, 2480a et seq. (1993). We will reverse and remand the district court's grant of judgment as a matter of law on those claims. Finally, we remand to the district court to determine whether Cushman has produced evidence sufficient to justify an award of punitive damages and to avoid preemption of her defamation claim.

I.

To the extent the facts are disputed, we view them in the light most favorable to Cushman. Cushman has a permanent residence in Pennsylvania but attended college in Vermont during the time period pertinent to this litigation. In the summer of 1993, an unknown person, possibly a member of her household in Philadelphia, applied under Cushman's name for credit cards from three credit grantors: American Express ("Amex"), Citibank Visa ("Citibank"), and Chase Manhattan Bank ("Chase"). The person provided the credit grantors with Cushman's social security number, address, and other identifying information. Credit cards were issued to that person in Cushman's name, and that person accumulated balances totaling approximately $2400 on the cards between June of 1993 and April of 1994. All this occurred without Cushman's knowledge.

In August of 1994, an unidentified bill collector informed Cushman that TUC was publishing a consumer credit report indicating that she was delinquent on payments to these three credit grantors. Cushman notified TUC that she had not applied for or used the three credit cards in question, and suggested that a third party had fraudulently applied for and obtained the cards. In response, a TUC clerk called Amex and Chase to inquire whether the verifying information (such as Cushman's name, social security number, and address) in Amex's and Chase's records matched the information in the TUC report. The TUC clerk also asked if Cushman had opened a fraud investigation with the credit grantors. Because the information matched, and because Cushman had not opened a fraud investigation, the information remained in the TUC report. TUC was unable to contact Citibank so TUC deleted the Citibank entry from the report. TUC's investigations are performed by clerks paid $7.50 per hour and who are expected to perform ten investigations per hour.

There is no evidence that TUC took the necessary steps to obtain access to pertinent documents from the credit grantors that would enable TUC to perform a handwriting comparison. TUC did allow Cushman the opportunity to complete a form requesting that a special handling statement be placed on her report, and that form required her signature. However, a TUC employee testified that the form would not have been used for a handwriting comparison had Cushman completed it. TUC advises consumers in Cushman's position to communicate with the credit grantors and complete signature verifications and affidavits of fraud with the credit grantors.

Cushman was sent a copy of the updated report still containing the Amex and Chase delinquencies. She sent a second letter to TUC reiterating her disagreement with the facts contained in the report and offering to sign affidavits for TUC to the effect that the delinquencies were not hers. TUC subsequently performed a reinvestigation identical to the first one but did nothing more. The credit report was not changed. At no time did TUC provide Cushman with a description of its reinvestigation procedures.

Cushman brought this action in the district court alleging negligent and willful failure to reinvestigate the disputed entries in violation of sections 611(a), 616, and 617 of the FCRA, 15

U.S.C. 1681i(a), 1681n, 1681o; violations of the VFCRA, VT. STAT. ANN. tit. 9, 2480a et seq.; and defamation. Subsequently, in April of 1995, TUC verified the information with Citibank, and placed the Citibank entry back onto Cushman's report. TUC notified Cushman of the reinsertion through her attorneys.

That September, Cushman for the first time disputed the delinquencies with the three credit grantors. A Citibank employee, comparing a handwriting sample provided by Cushman with the credit card application, determined that the card had been fraudulently obtained. The other two credit grantors came to a similar conclusion. TUC has since deleted the entries from Cushman's report.

TUC subsequently moved for summary judgment pursuant to Fed. R. Civ. P. 56, raising several issues addressed by this appeal. The district court denied the motion. See Cushman v. Trans Union Corp., 920 F. Supp. 80, 83-84 (E.D. Pa. 1996). However, at the close of Cushman's presentation of her case at trial, the district court sua sponte granted TUC judgment as a matter of law pursuant to Fed. R. Civ. P. 50(a) on all claims. Cushman timely appealed.

II.

A.

As this Court recently wrote:

The FCRA was enacted in order to ensure that

"consumer reporting agencies adopt reasonable procedures for meeting the needs of commerce for consumer credit, personnel, insurance, and other information in a manner which is fair and equitable to the consumer, with regard to the confidentiality, accuracy, relevancy, and proper utilization of such information." The FCRA was prompted by "congressional concern over abuses in the credit reporting industry." In the FCRA, Congress has recognized the crucial role that consumer reporting agencies play in collecting and transmitting consumer credit information, and the detrimental effects inaccurate information can visit upon both the individual consumer and the nation's economy as a whole.

Philbin v. Trans Union Corp., 101 F.3d 957, 962 (3d Cir. 1996) (quoting 15 U.S.C. 1681(b) and Guimond v. Trans Union Credit Information Co., 45 F.3d 1329, 1333 (9th Cir. 1995)) (citations omitted).

Title 15 U.S.C. 1681i(a) provides in relevant part:

If the completeness or accuracy of any item of information contained in [her] file is disputed by a consumer, and such dispute is directly conveyed to the consumer reporting agency by the consumer, the Consumer-reporting agency shall within a reasonable period of time reinvestigate and record the current status of that information unless it has reasonable grounds to believe that the dispute by the consumer is frivolous or irrelevant. If after such reinvestigation such information is found to be inaccurate or can no longer be verified, the consumer reporting agency shall promptly delete such information.

"Sections 1681n and 1681o of Title 15 respectively provide private rights of action for willful and negligent noncompliance with any duty imposed by the FCRA and allow recovery for actual damages and attorneys' fees and costs, as well as punitive damages in the case of willful noncompliance." Philbin, 101 F.3d at 962.1

---

1. *The Fair Credit Reporting Act has since been amended, effective September 30, 1997, by the Consumer Credit Reporting Reform Act of 1996, Pub. Law 104-208, Div. A, Title II, 2401 et seq., 110 Stat. 3009, ___-___. The amendments are not relevant to the issues raised in this appeal.*

1.

As an initial matter, we reject the suggestion made by TUC that no cause of action lies pursuant to 1681i(a) on the ground that 1681i(b) and (c) provide the exclusive remedy when a consumer disputes information that has been placed on her credit report. Those subsections provide that in the event a dispute under subsection (a) is not resolved, "the consumer may file a brief statement setting forth the nature of the dispute," 15 U.S.C. 1681i(b), and the statement or a summary must be included in the consumer's credit report. See 15 U.S.C. 1681i(c).

Subsections (b) and (c) have not been read as providing the exclusive remedy for a consumer in Cushman's position. See Henson v. CSC Credit Servs., 29 F.3d 280, 286 (7th Cir. 1994); Cahlin v. General Motors Acceptance Corp., 936 F.2d 1151, 1160 (11th Cir. 1991); Pinner v. Schmidt, 805 F.2d 1258, 1261-62 (5th Cir. 1986); see also Guimond, 45 F.3d at 1335 (dictum); cf. Thompson v. San Antonio Retail Merchants Assoc., 682 F.2d 509, 514-15 (5th Cir. 1982) (consumer need not pursue remedies under 1681i before suing under 1681e). The obligations prescribed by subsections (b) and (c) are triggered only after "the reinvestigation [pursuant to subsection (a)] does not resolve the dispute." 15 U.S.C. 1681i(b). This presupposes that a reasonable reinvestigation has already been completed and the dispute nonetheless remains unresolved. See Guimond, 45 F.3d at 1335. A consumer alleging that no reasonable reinvestigation has taken place has a separate claim pursuant to 1681i(a).

2.

We now turn to the questions of a consumer reporting agency's obligations pursuant to 1681i(a) and a plaintiff's burden of proving a claim of negligent noncompliance with that section. TUC contends that 1681i(a) did not impose on it an obligation to do any more than perform the reinvestigation it performed in this case. That is, TUC believes that when a consumer informs a consumer reporting agency that information contained in her consumer report is inaccurate, the consumer reporting agency is obliged only to confirm the accuracy of the information with the original source of the information. According to TUC, it is never required to go beyond the original source in ascertaining whether the information is accurate.

This position has been rejected by the United States Courts of Appeals for the Fifth and Seventh Circuits. See Henson, 29 F.3d at 286-87; Stevenson v. TRW Inc., 987 F.2d 288, 293 (5th Cir. 1993). In Henson, a state court judgment docket erroneously stated that an outstanding judgment had been entered against the plaintiff. Two credit reporting agencies included the erroneous entry on their consumer reports regarding the plaintiff. See Henson, 29 F.3d at 282-83. The plaintiff sued those credit reporting agencies pursuant to both 1681e(b) and 1681i. See id. at 284, 286. Section 1681e(b) requires consumer reporting agencies "to follow `reasonable procedures to assure maximum possible accuracy' of the information" contained in the credit report. Id. at 284 (quoting 15 U.S.C. 1681e(b))

The Seventh Circuit upheld the district court's dismissal of the 1681e(b) claim. See id. at 285-86. However, the court reversed the district court's dismissal of the 1681i claim, distinguishing between the duties imposed by the two sections of the statute. It stated:

A credit reporting agency that has been notified of potentially inaccurate information in a consumer's credit report is in a very different position than one who has no such notice. . . . [A] credit reporting agency may initially rely on public court documents, because to require otherwise would be burdensome and inefficient. However, such exclusive reliance may not be justified once the credit reporting agency receives notice that the consumer disputes information contained in his credit report. When a credit reporting agency receives such notice, it can target its resources in a more efficient manner and conduct a more thorough investigation.

Id. at 286-87 (emphasis added).

The Fifth Circuit came to a similar conclusion in Stevenson, 987 F.2d at 293. In that case, similar to the situation here, the consumer's son had fraudulently obtained accounts in the consumer's name. See id. at 291. Other inaccurate information appeared on the credit report as well. See id. The credit reporting agency sent written forms to the credit granting agencies that had originally supplied information concerning the consumer, and relied on those credit grantors to make the conclusive determination of whether the information was accurate. See id. at 293. Holding that this was insufficient, the court wrote: "In a reinvestigation of the accuracy of credit reports [pursuant to 1681i(a)], a credit bureau must bear some responsibility for evaluating the accuracy of information obtained from subscribers." Id. (citing Swoager v. Credit Bureau of Greater St. Petersburg, 608 F. Supp. 972, 976 (M.D. Fla. 1985)).

The court reasoned that such a result was the only one consistent with the language of 1681i(a), which requires "that the `consumer reporting agency shall within a reasonable period of time reinvestigate' and `promptly delete' inaccurate or unverifiable information." Id. (quoting 15 U.S.C. 1681i(a)) (emphasis in Stevenson). The court expressly rejected the same argument made here by TUC: "that where fraud has occurred, the consumer must resolve the problem with the creditor." Id. Rather, "[t]he statute places the burden of investigation squarely on" the consumer reporting agency. Id.

We agree with the conclusions reached by these courts. We assume for the sake of argument, as the Seventh Circuit concluded, that the costs of requiring consumer reporting agencies to go beyond the original source of information as an initial matter outweigh any potential benefits of such a requirement. Thus, we can assume that absent any indication that the information is inaccurate, the statute does not mandate such an investigation. However, as the Henson court explained, once a claimed inaccuracy is pinpointed, a consumer reporting agency conducting further investigation incurs only the cost of reinvestigating that one piece of disputed information. In short, when one goes from the 1681e(b) investigation to the 1681i(a) reinvestigation, the likelihood that the cost-benefit analysis will shift in favor of the consumer increases markedly. Judgment as a matter of law, even if appropriate on a 1681e(b) claim, thus may not be warranted on a 1681i(a) claim.

We also agree with the cogent observation by the Fifth

Circuit that the plain language of the statute places the burden of reinvestigation on the consumer reporting agency. See Stevenson, 987 F.2d at 293. The FCRA evinces Congress's intent that consumer reporting agencies, having the opportunity to reap profits through the collection and dissemination of credit information, bear "grave responsibilities," 15 U.S.C. 1681(a)(4), to ensure the accuracy of that information. The "grave responsibilit[y]" imposed by 1681i(a) must consist of something more than merely parroting information received from other sources. Therefore, a "reinvestigation" that merely shifts the burden back to the consumer and the credit grantor cannot fulfill the obligations contemplated by the statute.

In addition to these observations, we note that TUC's reading of 1681i(a) would require it only to replicate the efforts it must undertake in order to comply with 1681e(b). Such a reading would render the two sections largely duplicative of each other. We strive to avoid a result that would render statutory language superfluous, meaningless, or irrelevant. See Sekula v. F.D.I.C., 39 F.3d 448, 454 n.14 (3d Cir. 1994); Pennsylvania Dept. of Public Welfare v. United States Dept. of Health and Human Servs., 928 F.2d 1378, 1385 (3d Cir. 1991).

TUC contends that Podell v. Citicorp Diners Club, Inc., Nos. 96-7246, 314, 1997 WL 220320 (2d Cir. May 5, 1997), compels that we affirm. TUC is mistaken. In Podell, after being notified by a consumer of a dispute, a consumer reporting agency had performed the same sort of perfunctory reinvestigation that TUC performed here. See id. at *3. As here, the consumer sued the consumer reporting agency pursuant to 15 U.S.C. 1681i. See id.2

---

2. Podell also concerned a claim against a different consumer reporting agency pursuant to 15 U.S.C. 1681e(b). That portion of the opinion is not relevant to our discussion.

However, the consumer in Podell did not contend that the extent of the reinvestigation was unreasonably narrow, as Cushman argues here. Rather, the consumer's position in that case was that the consumer reporting agency never sent him an updated credit report or any other notice that a reinvestigation had been performed. See id. Therefore, he argued, he never had an opportunity to place a statement of dispute in his file pursuant to 1681i(b) and (c). See id. As the consumer in Podell never took issue with the reasonableness of the scope of the consumer reporting agency's reinvestigation, the Court of Appeals for the Second Circuit had no occasion to address this issue.

We hold that in order to fulfill its obligation under 1681i(a) "a credit reporting agency may be required, in certain circumstances, to verify the accuracy of its initial source of information." Henson, 29 F.3d at 287. We further hold that "[w]hether the credit reporting agency has a duty to go beyond the original source will depend" on a number of factors. Id. One of these is "whether the consumer has alerted the reporting agency to the possibility that the source may be unreliable or the reporting agency itself knows or should know that the source is unreliable." Id. A second factor is "the cost of verifying the accuracy of the source versus the possible harm inaccurately reported information may cause the consumer." Id. Whatever considerations exist, it is for "the trier of fact [to] weigh the[se] factors in deciding whether [the defendant] violated the provisions of section 1681i." Id.

In this case, the district court initially denied TUC's motion for summary judgment and relied on Henson in doing so, stating:

> The scope of the agency's duty to reinvestigate depends upon (1) the cost of verifying the accuracy of the source versus the potential harm to the consumer; and (2) the extent of the information the credit reporting agency possesses. . . . Once the credit reporting agency receives . . . notice [from the consumer that the credit report is inaccurate] it may be required to conduct a more thorough investigation, one that requires it to make inquiries beyond the original source of the information. . . .
>
> . . . [T]he decisive inquiry is whether Trans Union could have determined that the accounts were opened fraudulently if it had reasonably investigated the matter.

Cushman, 920 F. Supp. at 83 (citing Henson, 29 F.3d at 286-87).

This was in accord with our holding today. However, after the close of plaintiff's case the court stated, without further elaboration:

> I have entertained the evidence in this case to this point, and I tell you I am not persuaded that the plaintiff has met [her] burden to this Court in any claim that is before it at this juncture.
>
> Based on that, I'm going to grant a 50(a) motion in favor of the defendant.

App. at 256-57. As far as we can tell, the evidence before the court on defendant's summary judgment motion was not materially different from the evidence produced at trial. Most importantly, there was evidence produced at trial concerning the inaccuracy of the information, Cushman's notification to TUC of the inaccuracy and the underlying fraud, the nature of TUC's reinvestigation and the costs incurred by it in performing that reinvestigation, and the damages suffered by Cushman.

A reasonable jury weighing this evidence in light of the factors identified in Henson and endorsed by us today could have rendered a verdict for Cushman. The jury could have concluded that after TUC was alerted to the accusation that the accounts were obtained fraudulently, and then confronted with the credit grantors' reiteration of the inaccurate information, TUC should have known that the credit grantors were "unreliable" to the extent that they had not been informed of the fraud. See Henson, 29 F.3d at 286; see also Pinner, 805

F.2d at 1262 (where consumer informed consumer reporting agency of his personal dispute with manager of credit grantor, it was unreasonable under 1681i(a) for consumer reporting agency to rely solely on manager for information); cf. Bryant v. TRW, Inc., 689 F.2d 72, 79 (6th Cir. 1982) (similar efforts insufficient under 1681e(b)). Similarly, the jury could have concluded that seventy-five cents per investigation was too little to spend when weighed against Cushman's damages. See Henson, 29 F.3d at 287. It was for "the trier of fact [to] weigh the[se] factors." Id. (emphasis added). The district court arrogated that role to itself, and in doing so, it erred. Therefore, the judgment of the istrict court granting judgment as a matter of law on Cushman's claim for egligent noncompliance with 1681i(a) will be reversed and remanded.

3.

Cushman also claims that she is entitled to punitive damages pursuant to 15 U.S.C. 1681n because TUC's alleged noncompliance with 1681i(a) was willful. "To show willful noncompliance with the FCRA, [Cushman] must show that [TUC] `knowingly and intentionally committed an act in conscious disregard for the rights of others,' but need not show `malice or evil motive.' " Philbin, 101 F.3d at 970 (quoting Pinner, 805 F.2d at 1263). The Fifth Circuit has held that "[o]nly defendants who have engaged in `willful misrepresentations or concealments' have committed a willful violation and are subject to punitive damages under 1681n." Stevenson, 987 F.2d at 294 (quoting Pinner, 805 F.2d at 1263). Other courts have allowed punitive damages in cases involving concealments or misrepresentations without necessarily limiting the availability of punitive damages to such cases. See, e.g., Millstone v. O'Hanlon Reports, Inc., 528 F.2d 829, 834 (8th Cir. 1976); Collins v. Retail Credit Co., 410 F. Supp. 924, 931-32 (E.D. Mich. 1976).

Although we decline to adopt the Fifth Circuit's holding in Stevenson, we conclude that to justify an award of punitive damages, a defendant's actions must be on the same order as willful concealments or misrepresentations. If Cushman can prove, as she argues, that TUC adopted its reinvestigation policy either knowing that policy to be in contravention of the rights possessed by consumers pursuant to the FCRA or in reckless disregard of whether the policy contravened those rights, she may be awarded punitive damages.

The district court concluded that Cushman had not made out a case even of negligent noncompliance with 1681i(a). It therefore did not consider whether she had shown TUC's alleged noncompliance to be willful. Because the district court is more intimately familiar with the record in this matter, it is better situated than we to determine whether Cushman has produced sufficient evidence for a reasonable jury to find willfulness on the part of TUC pursuant to the standards we have set forth above. Therefore we will remand to the district court for such a determination.

B.

Cushman also claims that TUC has violated the VFCRA.

Vermont Statutes Annotated Title 9, 2480d is similar to 15 U.S.C. 1681i, providing, in pertinent part:

(a) If the completeness or accuracy of any item of information contained in the consumer's file is disputed by the consumer and the consumer notifies the credit reporting agency directly of such dispute, the agency shall reinvestigate free of charge and record the current status of the disputed information on or before 30 business days after the date the agency receives notice from the consumer.

. . . .

(e) If, after a reinvestigation under subsection (a) of this section of any information disputed by the consumer, the information is found to be inaccurate or cannot be verified, the credit reporting agency shall promptly delete such information from the consumer's file. . . .

(f) If any information is deleted after a reinvestigation under subsection (a) of this section, the information may not be reinserted in the consumer's file after deletion unless the person who furnishes the information reinvestigates and states in writing or by electronic record to the agency that the information is complete and accurate. . . . Upon such reinvestigation and statement by the furnisher, the credit reporting agency shall promptly notify the consumer of any reinsertion.

(g) A credit reporting agency shall provide written
notice of the results of any reinvestigation under
this subsection [which] shall include:

. . . .

(5) a description of the procedure used to determine
the accuracy and completeness of the information,
including the name, business address, and, if
available, the telephone number of any person
contacted in connection with such information . . . .

1.

As a threshold matter, we must determine whether Cushman's
relation to the state of Vermont is sufficient to bestow on her
the protections of the VFCRA. Vermont Statutes Annotated
Title 9, section 2480a(1) defines "consumer" as "a natural
person residing in this state." Thus, we must determine,
pursuant to Vermont law, whether Cushman "resid[ed]" in that
state for purposes of the statute. We have stated that "the term
`resident' has no precise meaning. Rather, its definition varies
with each statutory usage." Government of Virgin Islands ex
rel. Bodin v. Brathwaite, 459 F.2d 543, 544 (3d Cir. 1972)
(citations omitted); see also Willenbrock v. Rogers, 255 F.2d
236, 237 (3d Cir. 1958); United States v. Stabler, 169 F.2d 995,
998 (3d Cir. 1948). Unfortunately, the word "residing" is not
defined in the VFCRA and we have uncovered no cases
addressing what constitutes residency for purposes of the
VFCRA.

It is perhaps telling that the Vermont legislature left the word "residing" undefined in the VFCRA. It could have rendered a technical definition of residency for these purposes as it has for state income tax purposes. See VT. STAT. ANN. tit. 32, 5811(11)(A). Alternatively, it could have issued guidelines for the use of a state agency or the courts to establish their own definition of residency for these purposes, as it has for purposes of determining who is entitled to lowered tuition rates at state-supported institutions of higher learning. See VT. STAT. ANN. tit.16, 2282, 2282a.

Because it did neither of these things, we conclude that the Vermont legislature intended "residing" in VT. STAT. ANN. tit. 9, 2480a(1) to have its common legal meaning. In ordinary legal parlance, residency merely means "living in a particular locality" but not necessarily with the intent to make that locality "a fixed and permanent home." BLACK'S LAW DICTIONARY 1308-09 (6th ed. 1990); see also Wolinsky v. Bradford Nat'l Bank, 34 B.R. 702, 704 (D. Vt. 1983) (pursuant to Vermont law, " `[d]omicile' . . . means living in a locality with the intent to make it a fixed and permanent home, while `residence' simply requires bodily presence as an inhabitant in a given place") (citation omitted); Piche v. Department of Taxes, 565 A.2d 1283, 1285 (Vt. 1989) (residence is something less than domicile); Walker v. Walker, 200 A.2d 267, 269 (Vt. 1964) (same). But cf. Bonneau v. Russell, 85 A.2d 569, 570 (Vt. 1952) (equating residency and domicile for purposes of VT. STAT. ANN. tit. 47, 2713).3 On the other hand, residency implies something more than "merely transitory in nature," such as the happenstance of passing through a state on one's way to some other destination.

BLACK'S LAW DICTIONARY at 1309 (defining "resident");
see also Guessefeldt v. McGrath, 342 U.S. 308, 312, 72 S.Ct.
338, 341 (1951) (residence, for purposes of Trading with the
Enemy Act of 1917, 50 U.S.C. App. 2(a) (1990), "implies
something more than mere physical presence and something
less than domicile").

Brathwaite is instructive in this regard. In that case, we
were charged with the task of interpreting the word
"resident" in V.I. CODE ANN . tit. 16, 291(a) (1995), in order
to determine whether the petitioner could bring a paternity
proceeding under that section. As in this case, we had little
guidance in that endeavor. We noted that "residence may be
taken to indicate merely one's momentary factual place of
abode." Brathwaite, 459 F.2d at 544. We held that physical
presence in a locality "coupled with [an] intent to remain there
for a measurable period of time," satisfied the statute's
requirement of residency. Id. at 544-45. We further concluded
that the four-month period during which the petitioner had
continuously lived in the Virgin Islands prior to the conclusion
of the trial in that case sufficed to confer resident status upon
her. See id. at 545. Thus, to be a resident of a locale, one need
intend to live there not permanently nor indefinitely, but only
"for a measurable period of time." Id. Moreover, presence for a
period as short as four months will suffice. See also Stabler,
169 F.2d at 998 (defendant's "presence in New Jersey over a
period of weeks . . . was sufficient to give him a residence in
New Jersey" for purposes of 8 U.S.C. 738(b) (repealed 1952),
relating to revocation of naturalization).

The record reflects that during the period that TUC

allegedly failed to fulfill its obligations pursuant to the VFCRA (roughly from the autumn of 1994 through the spring of 1995), Cushman was in her senior year at the University of Vermont in Burlington. See App. at 147-56. It appears that she had been living in Vermont at least since the summer of 1993, except for "a brief few days at the end of the summer." Id. at 148. Moreover, she still lived in Vermont at the time of trial, in the spring of 1996. See id. at 147. The jury could reasonably infer from the evidence that, at the time of TUC's alleged violation of the VFCRA, (1) Cushman had already lived in Vermont for over a year, and (2) she intended to remain in Vermont at least until she graduated from the University and perhaps indefinitely. Thus, there was sufficient evidence from which a reasonable jury could conclude that Cushman was "residing" in Vermont during the relevant time period, pursuant to the ordinary legal meaning of that term. A jury could therefore conclude that Cushman may invoke the protections of the VFCRA.[4]

---

3. *Bonneau v. Russell, 85 A.2d 569, 570 (Vt. 1952), has been criticized for "fail[ing] to recognize the distinction in Vermont law between residence and domicile." Wolinsky v. Bradford Nat'l Bank, 34 B.R. 702, 704 n.1 (D. Vt. 1983).*

---

4. *Burger King Corp. v. Rudzewicz, 471 U.S. 462, 105 S.Ct. 2174 (1985),and International Shoe Co. v. Washington, 326 U.S. 310, 66 S.Ct. 154 (1945), cited by TUC, are inapposite.*

The question raised is whether Cushman may invoke the
protections of a Vermont statute, regardless of
where the action is brought. This issue is entirely separate and
distinct from the question whether a state or federal court
located in Vermont would be able, consistent with due process
principles, to assert personal urisdiction over TUC.

2.

Cushman claims that TUC violated VT. S TAT. ANN. tit. 9,
2480d(f), by not "promptly notify[ing]" her of the
reinsertion of the Citibank entry. A TUC employee testified
that it did notify her through her attorneys, see App. at
223-24, and Cushman has pointed to no contrary evidence
in the record. Cushman claims that this notification
occurred only during discovery in this litigation and
therefore was not sufficiently "prompt[ ]" to satisfy
2480d(f). The record does not indicate when the
notification was made to Cushman's attorneys. Accordingly,
we cannot conclude as a matter of law that TUC fulfilled its
obligations pursuant to that section. The district court's grant of
judgment as a matter of law on this claim will be reversed and
remanded for a jury determination of whether the notification
was sufficiently prompt pursuant to 2480d(f).

3.

Cushman also claims that TUC violated VT. STAT. ANN. tit.
9, 2480d(g)(5), by not providing her with a description of

its reinvestigation procedures. There is evidence that TUC did fail in this regard. See App. at 224-26. Therefore Cushman's claim pursuant to that section of the VFCRA must stand, as must her claims under those portions of the VFCRA that merely duplicate the FCRA.5

---

5. *TUC contends that the VFCRA claim should be dismissed on the additional ground that Cushman proved no damages stemming from the alleged violation of that statute. TUC points to a "concession" by Cushman's counsel in the district court that Cushman has not "pointed to any damage evidence specifically [with regard] to" the Vermont statute. App. at 260. As we read this, however, it appears that counsel merely stated that any damages caused by the alleged violations of the VFCRA were identical to those caused by the alleged violations of the FCRA. Thus, TUC's contention that Cushman conceded away any claim that she was damaged by a violation of the VFCRA is meritless.*

C.

1.

The district court dismissed Cushman's defamation claim on the ground that she had not produced any evidence of malice and because the FCRA preempts state law defamation claims except where the plaintiff proves "malice or willful intent to injure" her. 15 U.S.C. 1681h(e); see Bloom v. I.C.

Sys., Inc., 972 F.2d 1067, 1069 (9th Cir. 1992); Thornton v. Equifax, Inc., 619 F.2d 700, 703 (8th Cir. 1980). The parties have assumed that a showing of "malice or willful intent to injure" pursuant to 1681h(e) is identical to proof of willfulness under 1681n. This is contrary to the holding of the United States Court of Appeals for the Eighth Circuit in Thornton, 619 F.2d at 706, that 1681h(e) establishes a "higher requirement of proof." However, because neither the parties nor the district court addressed this issue, we will assume without deciding that the requirements for the two showings are identical. We have explained above that we will remand to the district court for a determination of whether Cushman has produced evidence sufficient to justify a finding of willfulness on the part of TUC pursuant to 1681n. See Part II.A.3 supra. We must likewise remand for a determination of whether Cushman has produced evidence of "malice or willful intent to injure" sufficient to avoid preemption of her defamation claim pursuant to 1681h(e).

2.

The district court granted TUC judgment as a matter of law on Cushman's defamation claim on the alternative ground that she had not produced any evidence of publication. In order to prove defamation pursuant to Pennsylvania law,6 Cushman must prove, inter alia, publication of the defamatory matter by TUC. See 42 PA.

6. Neither party has argued that the defamation claim is governed by the laws of Vermont or any other jurisdiction. In the absence of such a contention, we apply the laws of the forum state. See Publicker Indus., Inc. v. Roman Ceramics Corp., 652 F.2d 340, 343 n.6 (3d Cir. 1981).

CONS. STAT. ANN. 8343(a)(2) (1982); U.S. Healthcare, Inc. v. Blue Cross of Greater Philadelphia, 898 F.2d 914, 923 (3d Cir. 1990); Ertel v. Patriot-News Co., 674 A.2d 1038, 1043 (Pa.), cert. denied, ___ U.S. #6D6D 6D#, 117 S.Ct. 512 (1996). Publication consists of the communication of the information to at least one person other than the person defamed. See Flaxman v. Burnett, 574 A.2d 1061, 1066 (Pa. Super. 1990).

A TUC employee testified that the allegedly defamatory information was published to Chase and Citibank. See App. at 222, 338-39. Moreover, Cushman testified that an unidentified bill collector initially informed her of the allegedly defamatory information, from which a jury could infer that the information had been published to him as well. See id. at 149. A reasonable jury could conclude that Cushman has satisfied the publication element of her defamation cause of action.7 Thus, this was not a proper basis upon which to grant TUC judgment as a matter of law on the defamation claim.

III.

The judgment of the district court will be reversed and remanded for further proceedings consistent with this opinion.

A True Copy:
Teste:

   Clerk of the United States Court of Appeals
   for the Third Circuit

---

7. *We express no opinion as to whether Cushman has set forth evidence sufficient to prove the other elements of her defamation claim.*

CHAPTER 7

IF YOU CAN'T REMOVE DISPUTED DEBT FOR A VALID REASON

USE STATEMENTS ON CREDIT REPORTS TO EXPLAIN, RECONSIDER BANKRUPTCY, OR NEGOTIATE DEBT WAY DOWN BY CONSIDERING BANKRUPTCY

If you have tried three times to remove bad credit items without success, you still have other good options.

You can use any or all of the following ways to improve your credit.

1. You have every right to place a statement on your credit report explaining why you paid late or could not

pay. Examples of an explanation include that you lost your job, you got sick, or your wife lost her job.

2. You can negotiate your debts way down and then pay them off. You must get in writing from the debtor that you dispute the charge and that in exchange for a certain amount (often 20% of the amount owed) they will (1) cancel your debt and give you a receipt as paid in full, and (2) agree to report to the credit bureau that your debt is paid in full and paid on time. That is, cancel and remove that you had ever paid late.

3. Bankruptcy is always the last resort. You should only consider bankruptcy if you cannot clean up your credit using this book.

Some people are afraid of bankruptcy, as they believe it would hurt their credit forever. This is not true. If you have huge debts compared to your income, it is often to your advantage to file bankruptcy.

Your credit will often improve shortly after bankruptcy. This is because you will not have any more debts due. So, if you are working and have income from your job, creditors will prefer to make you a loan than someone who is drowning in debts.

Think about it. Would you rather give a credit card to someone who owes thousands of dollars and is late on many payments, or give a loan to someone who has no loans.

Others fear bankruptcy because it is right to live up to your promises. Think about this. Banks and credit card companies borrow money at about three percent and then loan it out at five, ten or twenty percent. The huge markup is because they know that five percent of all debts are late or never paid. Yes, the banks and credit card companies know that you will file bankruptcy if you need to. The interest charged to you takes into account your right to file bankruptcy.

Many credit card companies give credit cards to anyone employed after they file bankruptcy. So, you can have a great credit report within 12 months.

To file bankruptcy and learn about how easy it is to file and the low costs involved, just contact a lawyer that handles bankruptcy every day. You can look in the yellow pages under "attorney" or "lawyer" to find ads for lawyers that just do bankruptcy work.

CHAPTER 8

COPY OF FAIR CREDIT REPORT

(Reprinted from Federal Trade Commission's full text of FCRA)

FAIR CREDIT REPORTING ACT

As a public service, the staff of the Federal Trade Commission (FTC) has prepared the following complete text of the Fair Credit Reporting Act (FCRA), 15 U.S.C. § 1681 et seq. Although staff generally followed the format of the U.S. Code as published by the Government Printing Office, the format of this text does differ in minor ways from the Code (and from West's U.S. Code Annotated). For example, this version uses FCRA section numbers (§§ 601-625) in the headings. (The relevant U.S. Code citation is included with each section heading and each reference to the FCRA in the text.)

This version of the FCRA is complete as of January 7, 2002. It includes the amendments to the FCRA set forth in the Consumer Credit Reporting Reform Act of 1996 (Public Law 104-208, the Omnibus Consolidated Appropriations Act for Fiscal Year 1997, Title II, Subtitle D, Chapter 1), Section 311 of the Intelligence Authorization for Fiscal Year 1998 (Public Law 105-107), the Consumer Reporting Employment Clarification Act of 1998 (Public Law 105-347), Section 506 of the Gramm-Leach-Bliley Act (Public Law 106-102), and

Sections 358(g) and 505(c) of the Uniting and Strengthening America by Providing Appropriate Tools Required to Intercept and Obstruct Terrorism Act of 2001 (USA PATRIOT Act) (Public Law 107-56).

TABLE OF CONTENTS

§ 601. Short title
This title may be cited as the Fair Credit Reporting Act.

§ 602. Congressional findings and statement of purpose [15 U.S.C. § 1681]

(a) Accuracy and fairness of credit reporting. The Congress makes the following findings:

    (1) The banking system is dependent upon fair and accurate credit reporting. Inaccurate credit reports directly impair the efficiency of the banking system, and unfair credit reporting methods undermine the public confidence, which is essential to the continued functioning of the banking system.

    (2) An elaborate mechanism has been developed for investigating and evaluating the credit worthiness, credit standing, credit capacity, character, and general reputation of consumers.

    (3) Consumer reporting agencies have assumed a vital role in assembling and evaluating consumer credit and other information on consumers.

(4) There is a need to insure that consumer reporting agencies exercise their grave responsibilities with fairness, impartiality, and a respect for the consumer's right to privacy.

(b) Reasonable procedures. It is the purpose of this title to require that consumer reporting agencies adopt reasonable procedures for meeting the needs of commerce for consumer credit, personnel, insurance, and other information in a manner which is fair and equitable to the consumer, with regard to the confidentiality, accuracy, relevancy, and proper utilization of such information in accordance with the requirements of this title.

§ 603. Definitions; rules of construction [15 U.S.C. § 1681a]

(a) Definitions and rules of construction set forth in this section are applicable for the purposes of this title.

(b) The term "person" means any individual, partnership, corporation, trust, estate, cooperative, association, government or governmental subdivision or agency, or other entity.

(c) The term "consumer" means an individual.

(d) Consumer report.

(1) In general. The term "consumer report" means any written, oral, or other communication of any information by a consumer reporting agency bearing on a consumer's credit worthiness, credit standing, credit capacity, character, general reputation, personal characteristics, or mode of living which is used or expected to be used or collected in whole or in part for the purpose of serving as a factor in establishing the consumer's eligibility for

(A) credit or insurance to be used primarily for personal, family, or household purposes;

(B) employment purposes; or

(C) any other purpose authorized under section 604 [§ 1681b].

(2) Exclusions. The term "consumer report" does not include

(A) any

(i) report containing information solely as to transactions or experiences between the consumer and the person making the report;

(ii) communication of that information among persons related by common ownership or affiliated by corporate control; or

(iii) communication of other information among persons related by common ownership or affiliated by corporate control, if it is clearly and conspicuously disclosed to the consumer that the information may be communicated among such persons and the consumer is given the opportunity, before the time that the information is initially communicated, to direct that such information not be communicated among such persons;

(B) any authorization or approval of a specific extension of credit directly or indirectly by the issuer of a credit card or similar device;

(C) any report in which a person who has been requested by a third party to make a specific extension of credit directly or indirectly to a consumer conveys his or her decision with respect to such request, if the third party advises the consumer of the name and address of the person to whom the request was made, and such person makes the disclosures to the consumer required under section 615 [§ 1681m]; or

(D) a communication described in subsection (o).

(e) The term "investigative consumer report" means a consumer report or portion thereof in which information on a consumer's character, general reputation, personal characteristics, or mode of living is obtained through personal interviews with neighbors, friends, or associates of the consumer reported on or with others with whom he is acquainted or who may have knowledge concerning any such items of information. However, such information shall not include specific factual information on a consumer's credit record obtained directly from a creditor of the consumer or from a consumer reporting agency when such information was obtained directly from a creditor of the consumer or from the consumer.

(f) The term "consumer reporting agency" means any person which, for monetary fees, dues, or on a cooperative nonprofit basis, regularly engages in whole or in part in the practice of assembling or evaluating consumer credit information or other information on consumers for the purpose of furnishing consumer reports to third parties, and which uses any means or facility of interstate commerce for the purpose of preparing or furnishing consumer reports.

(g) The term "file," when used in connection with information on any consumer, means all of the information on that consumer recorded and retained by a consumer reporting agency regardless of how the information is stored.

(h) The term "employment purposes" when used in connection with a consumer report means a report used for the purpose of evaluating a consumer for employment, promotion, reassignment or retention as an employee.

(i) The term "medical information" means information or records obtained, with the consent of the individual to whom it relates, from licensed physicians or medical practitioners, hospitals, clinics, or other medical or medically related facilities.

(j) Definitions relating to child support obligations.

    (1) Overdue support. The term "overdue support" has the meaning given to such term in section 666(e) of title 42 [Social Security Act, 42 U.S.C. § 666(e)].

    (2) State or local child support enforcement agency. The term "State or local child support enforcement agency" means a State or local agency which administers a State or local program for establishing and enforcing child support obligations.

(k) Adverse action.

    (1) Actions included. The term "adverse action"

        (A) has the same meaning as in section 701(d)(6) of the Equal Credit Opportunity Act; and

        (B) means

(i)   a denial or cancellation of, an increase in any charge for, or a reduction or other adverse or unfavorable change in the terms of coverage or amount of, any insurance, existing or applied for, in connection with the underwriting of insurance;

(ii)   a denial of employment or any other decision for employment purposes that adversely affects any current or prospective employee;

(iii)   a denial or cancellation of, an increase in any charge for, or any other adverse or unfavorable change in the terms of, any license or benefit described in section 604(a)(3)(D) [§ 1681b]; and

(iv)   an action taken or determination that is

(I) made in connection with an application that was made by, or a transaction that was initiated by, any consumer, or in connection with a review of an account under section 604(a)(3)(F)(ii)[§1681b]; and

(II) adverse to the interests of the consumer.

(2) Applicable findings, decisions, commentary, and orders. For purposes of any determination of whether an action is an adverse action under paragraph (1)(A), all appropriate final findings, decisions, commentary, and orders issued under section 701(d)(6) of the Equal Credit Opportunity Act by the Board of Governors of the Federal

Reserve System or any court shall apply.

(l) Firm offer of credit or insurance. The term "firm offer of credit or insurance" means any offer of credit or insurance to a consumer that will be honored if the consumer is determined, based on information in a consumer report on the consumer, to meet the specific criteria used to select the consumer for the offer, except that the offer may be further conditioned on one or more of the following:

(1) The consumer being determined, based on information in the consumer's application for the credit or insurance, to meet specific criteria bearing on credit worthiness or insurability, as applicable, that are established

(A) before selection of the consumer for the offer; and

(B) for the purpose of determining whether to extend credit or insurance pursuant to the offer.

(2) Verification

(A) that the consumer continues to meet the specific criteria used to select the consumer for the offer, by using information in a consumer report on the consumer, information in the consumer's application for the credit or insurance, or other information bearing on the credit worthiness or insurability of the consumer; or

(B) of the information in the consumer's application for the credit or insurance, to determine that the consumer meets the specific criteria bearing on credit worthiness or insurability.

(2) The consumer furnishing any collateral that is a requirement for the extension of the credit or insurance that was

(A) established before selection of the consumer for the offer of credit or insurance; and

(B) disclosed to the consumer in the offer of credit or insurance.

(m) Credit or insurance transaction that is not initiated by the consumer. The term "credit or insurance transaction that is not initiated by the consumer" does not include the use of a consumer report by a person with which the consumer has an account or insurance policy, for purposes of

(1) reviewing the account or insurance policy; or

(2) collecting the account.

(n) State. The term "State" means any State, the Commonwealth of Puerto Rico, the District of Columbia, and any territory or possession of the United States.

(o) Excluded communications. A communication is

described in this subsection if it is a communication

(1) that, but for subsection (d)(2)(D), would be an investigative consumer report;

(2) that is made to a prospective employer for the purpose of

    (A) procuring an employee for the employer; or

    (B) procuring an opportunity for a natural person to work for the employer;

(3) that is made by a person who regularly performs such procurement;

(4) that is not used by any person for any purpose other than a purpose described in subparagraph (A) or (B) of paragraph (2); and

(5) with respect to which

  (A) the consumer who is the subject of the communication

      (i)   consents orally or in writing to the nature and scope of the communication, before the collection of any information for the purpose of making the communication;

      (ii)   consents orally or in writing to the making

of the communication to a prospective employer, before the making of the communication; and

    (iii)   in the case of consent under clause (i) or (ii) given orally, is provided written confirmation of that consent by the person making the communication, not later than 3 business days after the receipt of the consent by that person;

(B) the person who makes the communication does not, for the purpose of making the communication, make any inquiry that if made by a prospective employer of the consumer who is the subject of the communication would violate any applicable Federal or State equal employment opportunity law or regulation; and

(C) the person who makes the communication

    (i)   discloses in writing to the consumer who is the subject of the communication, not later than 5 business days after receiving any request from the consumer for such disclosure, the nature and substance of all information in the consumer's file at the time of the request, except that the sources of any information that is acquired solely for use in making the communication and is actually used for no other purpose, need not be disclosed other than under appropriate discovery procedures in any court of competent jurisdiction in which an action is brought; and

(ii)   notifies the consumer who is the subject of the communication, in writing, of the consumer's right to request the information described in clause (i).

(p) Consumer reporting agency that compiles and maintains files on consumers on a nationwide basis. The term "consumer reporting agency that compiles and maintains files on consumers on a nationwide basis" means a consumer reporting agency that regularly engages in the practice of assembling or evaluating, and maintaining, for the purpose of furnishing consumer reports to third parties bearing on a consumer's credit worthiness, credit standing, or credit capacity, each of the following regarding consumers residing nationwide:

(1) Public record information.

(2) Credit account information from persons who furnish that information regularly and in the ordinary course of business.

§ 604. Permissible purposes of consumer reports [15 U.S.C. § 1681b]

(a) In general. Subject to subsection (c), any consumer

reporting agency may furnish a consumer report under the following circumstances and no other:

(1) In response to the order of a court having jurisdiction to issue such an order, or a subpoena issued in connection with proceedings before a Federal grand jury.

(2) In accordance with the written instructions of the consumer to whom it relates.

(3) To a person which it has reason to believe

(A) intends to use the information in connection with a credit transaction involving the consumer on whom the information is to be furnished and involving the extension of credit to, or review or collection of an account of, the consumer; or

(B) intends to use the information for employment purposes; or

(C) intends to use the information in connection with the underwriting of insurance involving the consumer; or

(D) intends to use the information in connection with a determination of the consumer's eligibility for a license or other benefit granted by a governmental instrumentality required by law to consider an applicant's financial responsibility or status; or

(E) intends to use the information, as a potential investor or servicer, or current insurer, in connection with a valuation of, or an assessment of the credit or prepayment risks associated with, an existing credit obligation; or

(F) otherwise has a legitimate business need for the information

    (i)   in connection with a business transaction that is initiated by the consumer; or

    (ii)   to review an account to determine whether the consumer continues to meet the terms of the account.

(4) In response to a request by the head of a State or local child support enforcement agency (or a State or local government official authorized by the head of such an agency), if the person making the request certifies to the consumer reporting agency that

(A) the consumer report is needed for the purpose of establishing an individual's capacity to make child support payments or determining the appropriate level of such payments;

(B) the paternity of the consumer for the child to which the obligation relates has been established or acknowledged by the consumer in accordance with State laws under which the obligation arises (if required by those laws);

(C) the person has provided at least 10 days' prior notice to the consumer whose report is requested, by certified or registered mail to the last known address of the consumer, that the report will be requested; and

(D) the consumer report will be kept confidential, will be used solely for a purpose described in subparagraph (A), and will not be used in connection with any other civil, administrative, or criminal proceeding, or for any other purpose.

(5) To an agency administering a State plan under Section 454 of the Social Security Act (42 U.S.C. § 654) for use to set an initial or modified child support award.

(b) Conditions for furnishing and using consumer reports for employment purposes.

(1) Certification from user. A consumer reporting agency may furnish a consumer report for employment purposes only if

(A) the person who obtains such report from the agency certifies to the agency that

(i)   the person has complied with paragraph (2) with respect to the consumer report, and the person will comply with paragraph (3) with respect to the consumer report if paragraph (3) becomes applicable; and

(ii)   information from the consumer report will not be used in violation of any applicable Federal or State equal employment opportunity law or regulation; and

(B) the consumer reporting agency provides with the report, or has previously provided, a summary of the consumer's rights under this title, as prescribed by the Federal Trade Commission under section 609(c)(3) [§ 1681g].

(2) Disclosure to consumer.

(A) In general. Except as provided in subparagraph (B), a person may not procure a consumer report, or cause a consumer report to be procured, for employment purposes with respect to any consumer, unless--

(i)   a clear and conspicuous disclosure has been made in writing to the consumer at any time before the report is procured or caused to be procured, in a document that consists solely of the disclosure, that a consumer report may be obtained for employment purposes; and

(ii)   the consumer has authorized in writing (which authorization may be made on the document referred to in clause (i)) the procurement of the report by that person.

(B) Application by mail, telephone, computer, or other similar means. If a consumer described in subparagraph (C) applies for employment by mail, telephone, computer, or other similar means, at any time before a consumer report is procured or caused to be procured in connection with that application--

    (i)   the person who procures the consumer report on the consumer for employment purposes shall provide to the consumer, by oral, written, or electronic means, notice that a consumer report may be obtained for employment purposes, and a summary of the consumer's rights under section 615(a)(3); and

    (ii)   the consumer shall have consented, orally, in writing, or electronically to the procurement of the report by that person.

(C) Scope. Subparagraph (B) shall apply to a person procuring a consumer report on a consumer in connection with the consumer's application for employment only if--

    (i)   the consumer is applying for a position over which the Secretary of Transportation has the power to establish qualifications and maximum hours of service pursuant to the provisions of section 31502 of title 49, or a position subject to safety regulation by a State transportation agency; and

(ii)   as of the time at which the person procures the report or causes the report to be procured the only interaction between the consumer and the person in connection with that employment application has been by mail, telephone, computer, or other similar means.

(3) Conditions on use for adverse actions.

(A) In general. Except as provided in subparagraph (B), in using a consumer report for employment purposes, before taking any adverse action based in whole or in part on the report, the person intending to take such adverse action shall provide to the consumer to whom the report relates--

(i)   a copy of the report; and

(ii)   a description in writing of the rights of the consumer under this title, as prescribed by the Federal Trade Commission under section 609(c)(3).

(B) Application by mail, telephone, computer, or other similar means.

(i) If a consumer described in subparagraph (C) applies for employment by mail, telephone, computer, or other similar means, and if a person who has procured a consumer report on the consumer for employment purposes takes adverse action on the employment application based in whole or in part on the report, then the person must provide to the consumer to whom the report relates, in lieu of the notices required under subparagraph (A) of this section and under section 615(a), within 3 business days of taking such action, an oral, written or electronic notification--

(I) that adverse action has been taken based in whole or in part on a consumer report received from a consumer reporting agency;

(II) of the name, address and telephone number of the consumer reporting agency that furnished the consumer report (including a toll-free telephone number established by the agency if the agency compiles and maintains files on consumers on a nationwide basis);

(III) that the consumer reporting agency did not make the decision to take the adverse action and is unable to provide to the consumer the specific reasons why the adverse action was taken; and

(IV) that the consumer may, upon providing proper identification, request a free copy of a report and may dispute with the consumer reporting agency the accuracy or completeness of any information in a report.

(ii) If, under clause (B)(i)(IV), the consumer requests a copy of a consumer report from the person who procured the report, then, within 3 business days of receiving the consumer's request, together with proper identification, the person must send or provide to the consumer a copy of a report and a copy of the consumer's rights as prescribed by the Federal Trade Commission under section 609(c)(3).

(C) Scope. Subparagraph (B) shall apply to a person procuring a consumer report on a consumer in connection with the consumer's application for employment only if--

(i) the consumer is applying for a position over which the Secretary of Transportation has the power to establish qualifications and maximum hours of service pursuant to the provisions of section 31502 of title 49, or a position subject to safety regulation by a State transportation agency; and

(ii)   as of the time at which the person procures the report or causes the report to be procured the only interaction between the consumer and the person in connection with that employment application has been by mail, telephone, computer, or other similar means.

(4) Exception for national security investigations.

(A) In general. In the case of an agency or department of the United States Government which seeks to obtain and use a consumer report for employment purposes, paragraph (3) shall not apply to any adverse action by such agency or department which is based in part on such consumer report, if the head of such agency or department makes a written finding that--

(i)   the consumer report is relevant to a national security investigation of such agency or department;

(ii)   the investigation is within the jurisdiction of such agency or department;

(iii)   there is reason to believe that compliance with paragraph (3) will--

(I) endanger the life or physical safety of any person;

(II) result in flight from prosecution;

(III) result in the destruction of, or tampering with, evidence relevant to the investigation;

(IV) result in the intimidation of a potential witness relevant to the investigation;

(V) result in the compromise of classified information; or

(VI) otherwise seriously jeopardize or unduly delay the investigation or another official proceeding.

(B) Notification of consumer upon conclusion of investigation. Upon the conclusion of a national security investigation described in subparagraph (A), or upon the determination that the exception under subparagraph (A) is no longer required for the reasons set forth in such subparagraph, the official exercising the authority in such subparagraph shall provide to the consumer who is the subject of the consumer report with regard to which such finding was made--

(i) a copy of such consumer report with any

classified information redacted as necessary;

    (ii)   notice of any adverse action which is based, in part, on the consumer report; and

    (iii)   the identification with reasonable specificity of the nature of the investigation for which the consumer report was sought.

(C) Delegation by head of agency or department. For purposes of subparagraphs (A) and (B), the head of any agency or department of the United States Government may delegate his or her authorities under this paragraph to an official of such agency or department who has personnel security responsibilities and is a member of the Senior Executive Service or equivalent civilian or military rank.

(D) Report to the congress. Not later than January 31 of each year, the head of each agency and department of the United States Government that exercised authority under this paragraph during the preceding year shall submit a report to the Congress on the number of times the department or agency exercised such authority during the year.

(E) Definitions. For purposes of this paragraph, the following definitions shall apply:

    (i)   Classified information. The term `classified

information' means information that is protected from unauthorized disclosure under Executive Order No. 12958 or successor orders.

(ii) National security investigation. The term national security investigation' means any official inquiry by an agency or department of the United States Government to determine the eligibility of a consumer to receive access or continued access to classified information or to determine whether classified information has been lost or compromised.

(c) Furnishing reports in connection with credit or insurance transactions that are not initiated by the consumer.

(1) In general. A consumer reporting agency may furnish a consumer report relating to any consumer pursuant to subparagraph (A) or (C) of subsection (a)(3) in connection with any credit or insurance transaction that is not initiated by the consumer only if

(A) the consumer authorizes the agency to provide such report to such person; or

(B) (i) the transaction consists of a firm offer of credit or insurance;

(ii) the consumer reporting agency has complied with subsection (e); and

(iii) there is not in effect an election by the consumer, made in accordance with subsection (e), to have the consumer's name and address excluded from lists of names provided by the agency pursuant to this paragraph.

(2) Limits on information received under paragraph (1)(B). A person may receive pursuant to paragraph (1)(B) only

(A) the name and address of a consumer;

(B) an identifier that is not unique to the consumer and that is used by the person solely for the purpose of verifying the identity of the consumer; and

(C) other information pertaining to a consumer that does not identify the relationship or experience of the consumer with respect to a particular creditor or other entity.

(3) Information regarding inquiries. Except as provided in section 609(a)(5) [§ 1681g], a consumer reporting agency shall not furnish to any person a record of inquiries in onnection with a credit or insurance transaction that is not initiated by a consumer.

(d) Reserved.

(e) Election of consumer to be excluded from lists.
  (1) In general. A consumer may elect to have the consumer's name and address excluded from any list provided by a consumer reporting agency under subsection (c)(1)(B) in connection with a credit or insurance transaction that is not initiated by the consumer, by notifying the agency in accordance with paragraph (2) that the consumer does not consent to any use of a consumer report relating to the consumer in connection with any credit or insurance transaction that is not initiated by the consumer.

  (2) Manner of notification. A consumer shall notify a consumer reporting agency under paragraph (1)

     (A) through the notification system maintained by the agency under paragraph (5); or

     (B) by submitting to the agency a signed notice of election form issued by the agency for purposes of this subparagraph.

  (3) Response of agency after notification through system. Upon receipt of notification of the election of a consumer under paragraph (1) through the notification system maintained by the agency under paragraph (5), a consumer reporting agency shall

     (A) inform the consumer that the election is effective only for the 2-year period following the election if the consumer does not submit to the agency a signed notice of election form issued by the agency for purposes of paragraph (2)(B); and

(B) provide to the consumer a notice of election form, if

(C) requested by the consumer, not later than 5 business days after receipt of the notification of the election through the system established under paragraph (5), in the case of a request made at the time the consumer provides notification through the system.

(4) Effectiveness of election. An election of a consumer under paragraph (1)

(A) shall be effective with respect to a consumer reporting agency beginning 5 business days after the date on which the consumer notifies the agency in accordance with paragraph (2);

(B) shall be effective with respect to a consumer reporting agency

(i) subject to subparagraph (C), during the 2-year period beginning 5 business days after the date on which the consumer notifies the agency of the election, in the case of an election for which a consumer notifies the agency only in accordance with paragraph (2)(A); or

(ii)   until the consumer notifies the agency under subparagraph (C), in the case of an election for which a consumer notifies the agency in accordance with paragraph (2)(B);

(C) shall not be effective after the date on which the consumer notifies the agency, through the notification system established by the agency under paragraph (5), that the election is no longer effective; and

(D) shall be effective with respect to each affiliate of the agency.

(5) Notification system.

(A) In general. Each consumer reporting agency that, under subsection (c)(1)(B), furnishes a consumer report in connection with a credit or insurance transaction that is not initiated by a consumer, shall

(i)   establish and maintain a notification system, including a toll-free telephone number, which permits any consumer whose consumer report is maintained by the agency to notify the agency, with appropriate identification, of the consumer's election to have the consumer's name and address excluded from any such list of names and addresses provided by the agency for such a transaction; and

(ii) publish by not later than 365 days after the date of enactment of the Consumer Credit Reporting Reform Act of 1996, and not less than annually thereafter, in a publication of general circulation in the area served by the agency

(I) a notification that information in consumer files maintained by the agency may be used in connection with such transactions; and

(II) the address and toll-free telephone number for consumers to use to notify the agency of the consumer's election under clause (I).

(B) Establishment and maintenance as compliance. Establishment and maintenance of a notification system (including a toll-free telephone number) and publication by a consumer reporting agency on the agency's own behalf and on behalf of any of its affiliates in accordance with this paragraph is deemed to be compliance with this paragraph by each of those affiliates.

(6) Notification system by agencies that operate nationwide. Each consumer reporting agency that compiles and maintains files on consumers on a nationwide basis shall establish and maintain a notification system for purposes of paragraph (5) jointly with other such consumer reporting agencies.

(f) Certain use or obtaining of information prohibited. A person shall not use or obtain a consumer report for any purpose unless

(1) the consumer report is obtained for a purpose for which the consumer report is authorized to be furnished under this section; and

(2) the purpose is certified in accordance with section 607 [§ 1681e] by a prospective user of the report through a general or specific certification.

(g) Furnishing reports containing medical information. A consumer reporting agency shall not furnish for employment purposes, or in connection with a credit or insurance transaction, a consumer report that contains medical information about a consumer, unless the consumer consents to the furnishing of the report.

§ 605. Requirements relating to information contained in consumer reports [15 U.S.C. § 1681c]

(a) Information excluded from consumer reports. Except as authorized under subsection (b) of this section, no consumer reporting agency may make any consumer report containing any of the following items of information:

(1) Cases under title 11 [United States Code] or under the Bankruptcy Act that, from the date of entry of the order for relief or the date of adjudication, as the case may be, antedate the report by more than 10 years.

(2) Civil suits, civil judgments, and records of arrest that from date of entry, antedate the report by more than seven years or until the governing statute of limitations has expired, whichever is the longer period.

(3) Paid tax liens which, from date of payment, antedate the report by more than seven years.

(4) Accounts placed for collection or charged to profit and loss which antedate the report by more than seven years.(1)

(5) Any other adverse item of information, other than records of convictions of crimes which antedates the report by more than seven years.1

(b) Exempted cases. The provisions of subsection (a) of this section are not applicable in the case of any consumer credit report to be used in connection with
(1) a credit transaction involving, or which may reasonably

be expected to involve, a principal amount of $150,000 or more;

(2) the underwriting of life insurance involving, or which may reasonably be expected to involve, a face amount of $150,000 or more; or

(3) the employment of any individual at an annual salary which equals, or which may reasonably be expected to equal $75,000, or more.

(c) Running of reporting period.

(1) In general. The 7-year period referred to in paragraphs (4) and (6)(2) of subsection (a) shall begin, with respect to any delinquent account that is placed for collection (internally or by referral to a third party, whichever is earlier), charged to profit and loss, or subjected to any similar action, upon the expiration of the 180-day period beginning on the date of the commencement of the delinquency which immediately preceded the collection activity, charge to profit and loss, or similar action.

(2) Effective date. Paragraph (1) shall apply only to items of information added to the file of a consumer on or after the date that is 455 days after the date of enactment of the Consumer Credit Reporting Reform Act of 1996.

(d) Information required to be disclosed. Any consumer

reporting agency that furnishes a consumer report that contains information regarding any case involving the consumer that arises under title 11, United States Code, shall include in the report an identification of the chapter of such title 11 under which such case arises if provided by the source of the information. If any case arising or filed under title 11, United States Code, is withdrawn by the consumer before a final judgment, the consumer reporting agency shall include in the report that such case or filing was withdrawn upon receipt of documentation certifying such withdrawal.

(e) Indication of closure of account by consumer. If a consumer reporting agency is notified pursuant to section 623(a)(4) [§ 1681s-2] that a credit account of a consumer was voluntarily closed by the consumer, the agency shall indicate that fact in any consumer report that includes information related to the account.

(f) Indication of dispute by consumer. If a consumer reporting agency is notified pursuant to section 623(a)(3) [§ 1681s-2] that information regarding a consumer who was furnished to the agency is disputed by the consumer, the agency shall indicate that fact in each consumer report that includes the disputed information.

§ 606. Disclosure of investigative consumer reports [15 U.S.C. § 1681d]

(a) Disclosure of fact of preparation. A person may not procure or cause to be prepared an investigative consumer report on any consumer unless

(1) it is clearly and accurately disclosed to the consumer that an investigative consumer report including information as to his character, general reputation, personal characteristics and mode of living, whichever are applicable, may be made, and such disclosure

   (A) is made in a writing mailed, or otherwise delivered, to the consumer, not later than three days after the date on which the report was first requested, and

   (B) includes a statement informing the consumer of his right to request the additional disclosures provided for under subsection (b) of this section and the written summary of the rights of the consumer prepared pursuant to section 609(c) [§ 1681g]; and

(2) the person certifies or has certified to the consumer reporting agency that

   (A) the person has made the disclosures to the consumer required by paragraph (1); and

   (B) the person will comply with subsection (b).

(b) Disclosure on request of nature and scope of investigation. Any person who procures or causes to be prepared an investigative consumer report on any consumer shall, upon written request made by the consumer within a reasonable period of time after the receipt by him of the disclosure required by subsection (a)(1) of this section, make a complete and accurate disclosure of the nature and scope of the investigation requested. This disclosure shall be made in a writing mailed, or otherwise delivered, to the consumer not later than five days after the date on which the request for such disclosure was received from the consumer or such report was first requested, whichever is the later.

(c) Limitation on liability upon showing of reasonable procedures for compliance with provisions. No person may be held liable for any violation of subsection (a) or (b)of this section if he shows by a preponderance of the evidence that at the time of the violation he maintained reasonable procedures to assure compliance with subsection (a) or (b) of this section.

(d) Prohibitions.

(1) Certification. A consumer reporting agency shall not prepare or furnish investigative consumer report unless the agency has received a certification under subsection (a)(2) from the person who requested the report.

(2) Inquiries. A consumer reporting agency shall not make an inquiry for the purpose of preparing an investigative consumer report on a consumer for employment purposes if the making of the inquiry by an employer or prospective employer of the

consumer would violate any applicable Federal or State equal employment opportunity law or regulation.

(3) Certain public record information. Except as otherwise provided in section 613 [§ 1681k], a consumer reporting agency shall not furnish an investigative consumer report that includes information that is a matter of public record and that relates to an arrest, indictment, conviction, civil judicial action, tax lien, or outstanding judgment, unless the agency has verified the accuracy of the information during the 30-day period ending on the date on which the report is furnished.

(4) Certain adverse information. A consumer reporting agency shall not prepare or furnish an investigative consumer report on a consumer that contains information that is adverse to the interest of the consumer and that is obtained through a personal interview with a neighbor, friend, or associate of the consumer or with another person with whom the consumer is acquainted or who has knowledge of such item of information, unless

(A) the agency has followed reasonable procedures to obtain confirmation of the information, from an additional source that has independent and direct knowledge of the information; or

(B) the person interviewed is the best possible source of the information.

§ 607. Compliance procedures [15 U.S.C. § 1681e]

(a) Identity and purposes of credit users. Every consumer reporting agency shall maintain reasonable procedures designed to avoid violations of section 605 [§ 1681c] and to limit the furnishing of consumer reports to the purposes listed under section 604 [§ 1681b] of this title. These procedures shall require that prospective users of the information identify themselves, certify the purposes for which the information is sought, and certify that the information will be used for no other purpose. Every consumer reporting agency shall make a reasonable effort to verify the identity of a new prospective user and the uses certified by such prospective user prior to furnishing such user a consumer report. No consumer reporting agency may furnish a consumer report to any person if it has reasonable grounds for believing that the consumer report will not be used for a purpose listed in section 604 [§ 1681b] of this title.

(b) Accuracy of report. Whenever a consumer reporting agency prepares a consumer report it shall follow reasonable procedures to assure maximum possible accuracy of the information concerning the individual about whom the report relates.

(c) Disclosure of consumer reports by users allowed. A

consumer reporting agency may not prohibit a user of a consumer report furnished by the agency on a consumer from disclosing the contents of the report to the consumer, if adverse action against the consumer has been taken by the user based in whole or in part on the report.

(d) Notice to users and furnishers of information.

(1) Notice requirement. A consumer reporting agency shall provide to any person

(A) who regularly and in the ordinary course of business furnishes information to the agency with respect to any consumer; or

(B) to whom a consumer report is provided by the agency;

a notice of such person's responsibilities under this title.

(2) Content of notice. The Federal Trade Commission shall prescribe the content of notices under paragraph (1), and a consumer reporting agency shall be in compliance with this subsection if it provides a notice under paragraph (1) that is substantially similar to the Federal Trade Commission prescription under this paragraph.

(e) Procurement of consumer report for resale.

(1) Disclosure. A person may not procure a consumer

report for purposes of reselling the report (or any information in the report) unless the person discloses to the consumer reporting agency that originally furnishes the report

(A) the identity of the end-user of the report (or information); and

(B) each permissible purpose under section 604 [§1681b] for which the report is furnished to the end-user of the report (or information).

   (2) Responsibilities of procurers for resale. A person who procures a consumer report for purposes of reselling the report (or any information in report) shall

(A) establish and comply with reasonable procedures designed to ensure that the report (or information) is resold by the person only for a purpose for which the report may be furnished under section 604 [§1681b], including by requiring that each person to which the report (or information) is resold and that resells or provides the report (or information) to any other person

      (i) identifies each end user of the resold report (or information);

      (ii) certifies each purpose for which the report (or information) will be used; and

          (iii) certifies that the report (or information) will be used for no other purpose; and

   (B) before reselling the report, make reasonable efforts to verify the identifications and certifications made under subparagraph (A).

      (3) Resale of consumer report to a federal agency or department. Notwithstanding paragraph (1) or (2), a person who procures a consumer report for purposes of reselling the report (or any information in the report) shall not disclose the identity of the end-user of the report under paragraph (1) or (2) if-

   (A) the end user is an agency or department of the United States Government which procures the report from the person for purposes of determining the eligibility of the consumer concerned to receive access or continued access to classified information (as defined in section 604(b)(4)(E)(i)); and

   (B) the agency or department certifies in writing to the person reselling the report that nondisclosure is necessary to protect classified information or the safety of persons employed by or contracting with, undergoing investigation for work or contracting with the agency or department.

   § 608. Disclosures to governmental agencies [15 U.S.C. § 1681f]

Notwithstanding the provisions of section 604 [§ 1681b] of this title, a consumer reporting agency may furnish identifying information respecting any consumer, limited to his name, address, former addresses, places of employment, or former places of employment, to a governmental agency.

§ 609. Disclosures to consumers [15 U.S.C. § 1681g]

(a) Information on file; sources; report recipients. Every consumer reporting agency shall, upon request, and subject to 610(a)(1) [§ 1681h], clearly and accurately disclose to the consumer:

(1) All information in the consumer's file at the time of the request, except that nothing in this paragraph shall be construed to require a consumer reporting agency to disclose to a consumer any information concerning credit scores or any other risk scores or predictors relating to the consumer.

(2) The sources of the information; except that the sources of information acquired solely for use in preparing an investigative consumer report and actually used for no other purpose need not be disclosed: Provided, That in the event an action is brought under this title, such sources shall be available to the plaintiff under appropriate discovery procedures in the court in which the action is brought.

(3)(A) Identification of each person (including each end-user identified under section 607(e)(1) [§ 1681e]) that procured a consumer report

    (i)   for employment purposes, during the 2-year period preceding the date on which the request is made; or

    (ii)   for any other purpose, during the 1-year period preceding the date on which the request is made.

(B) An identification of a person under subparagraph (A) shall include

    (i)   the name of the person or, if applicable, the trade name (written in full) under which such person conducts business; and

    (ii)   upon request of the consumer, the address and telephone number of the person.

(C) Subparagraph (A) does not apply if--

    (i)   the end user is an agency or department of the United States Government that procures the report from the person for purposes of determining the eligibility of the consumer to whom the report relates to receive access or continued access to classified information (as defined in section 604(b)(4)(E)(i)); and

    (ii)   the head of the agency or department makes a written finding as prescribed under section

604(b)(4)(A).

(3) The dates, original payees, and amounts of any checks upon which is based any adverse characterization of the consumer, included in the file at the time of the disclosure.

(4) A record of all inquiries received by the agency during the 1-year period preceding the request that identified the consumer in connection with a credit or insurance transaction that was not initiated by the consumer.

(b) Exempt information. The requirements of subsection (a) of this section respecting the disclosure of sources of information and the recipients of consumer reports do not apply to information received or consumer reports furnished prior to the effective date of this title except to the extent that the matter involved is contained in the files of the consumer reporting agency on that date.

(c) Summary of rights required to be included with disclosure.

(1) Summary of rights. A consumer reporting agency shall provide to a consumer, with each written disclosure by the agency to the consumer under this section

(A) a written summary of all of the rights that the consumer has under this title; and

(B) in the case of a consumer reporting agency that compiles and maintains files on consumers on a nationwide basis, a toll-free telephone number established by the agency, at which personnel are accessible to consumers during normal business hours.

(2) Specific items required to be included. The summary of rights required under paragraph (1) shall include

(A) a brief description of this title and all rights of consumers under this title;

(B) an explanation of how the consumer may exercise the rights of the consumer under this title;

(C) a list of all Federal agencies responsible for enforcing any provision of this title and the address and any appropriate phone number of each such agency, in a form that will assist the consumer in selecting the appropriate agency;

(D) a statement that the consumer may have additional rights under State law and that the consumer may wish to contact a State or local consumer protection agency or a State attorney general to learn of those rights; and

(E) a statement that a consumer reporting agency is not required to remove accurate derogatory information from a consumer's file, unless the information is outdated under section 605 [§ 1681c] or cannot be verified.

(3) Form of summary of rights. For purposes of this subsection and any disclosure by a consumer reporting agency required under this title with respect to consumers' rights, the Federal Trade Commission (after consultation with each Federal agency referred to in section 621(b) [§1681s]) shall prescribe the form and content of any such disclosure of the rights of consumers required under this title. A consumer reporting agency shall be in compliance with this subsection if it provides disclosures under paragraph (1) that are substantially similar to the Federal Trade Commission prescription under this paragraph.

(4) Effectiveness. No disclosures shall be required under this subsection until the date on which the Federal Trade Commission prescribes the form and content of such disclosures under paragraph (3).

§ 610. Conditions and form of disclosure to consumers [15 U.S.C. § 1681h]

(a) In general.

(1) Proper identification. A consumer reporting agency shall require, as a condition of making the disclosures required under section 609 [§ 1681g], that the consumer furnish proper identification.

(2) Disclosure in writing. Except as provided in subsection (b), the disclosures required to be made under section 609 [§ 1681g] shall be provided under that section in writing.

(b) Other forms of disclosure.

(1) In general. If authorized by a consumer, a consumer reporting agency may make the disclosures required under 609 [§ 1681g]

(A) other than in writing; and

(B) in such form as may be

(i) specified by the consumer in accordance with paragraph (2); and

(ii) available from the agency.

(2) Form. A consumer may specify pursuant to paragraph (1) that disclosures under section 609 [§ 1681g] shall be made

(A) in person, upon the appearance of the consumer at the place of business of the consumer reporting agency where disclosures are regularly provided, during normal business hours, and on reasonable notice;

(B) by telephone, if the consumer has made a written request for disclosure by telephone;

(C) by electronic means, if available from the agency; or

(D) by any other reasonable means that is available from the agency.

(c) Trained personnel. Any consumer reporting agency shall provide trained personnel to explain to the consumer any information furnished to him pursuant to section 609 [§ 1681g] of this title.

(d) Persons accompanying consumer. The consumer shall be permitted to be accompanied by one other person of his choosing, who shall furnish reasonable identification. A consumer reporting agency may require the consumer to furnish a written statement granting permission to the consumer reporting agency to discuss the consumer's file in such person's presence.

(e) Limitation of liability. Except as provided in sections 616 and 617 [§§1681n and 1681o] of this title, no consumer may bring any action or proceeding in the nature of defamation, invasion of privacy, or negligence with respect to the reporting of information against any consumer reporting agency, any user of information, or any person who furnishes information to a consumer reporting agency, based on information disclosed pursuant to section 609, 610, or 615 [§§ 1681g, 1681h, or 1681m] of this title or based on information disclosed by a user of a consumer report to or for a consumer against whom the user has taken adverse action, based in whole or in part on the report, except as to false information furnished with malice or willful intent to injure such consumer.

§ 611. Procedure in case of disputed accuracy [15 U.S.C. § 1681i]

(a) Reinvestigations of disputed information.

(1) Reinvestigation required.

(A) In general. If the completeness or accuracy of any item of information contained in a consumer's file at a consumer reporting agency is disputed by the consumer and the consumer notifies the agency directly of such dispute, the agency shall reinvestigate free of charge and record the current status of the disputed information, or delete the item from the file in accordance with paragraph (5), before the end of the 30-day period beginning on the date on which the agency receives the notice of the dispute from the consumer.

(B) Extension of period to reinvestigate. Except as provided in subparagraph (C), the 30-day period described in subparagraph (A) may be extended for not more than 15 additional days if the consumer reporting agency receives information from the consumer during that 30-day period that is relevant to the reinvestigation.

(C) Limitations on extension of period to reinvestigate.

Subparagraph (B) shall not apply to any reinvestigation in which, during the 30-day period described in subparagraph (A), the information that is the subject of the reinvestigation is found to be inaccurate or incomplete or the consumer reporting agency determines that the information cannot be verified.

(2) Prompt notice of dispute to furnisher of information.

(A) In general. Before the expiration of the 5-business-day period beginning on the date on which a consumer reporting agency receives notice of a dispute from any consumer in accordance with paragraph (1), the agency shall provide notification of the dispute to any person who provided any item of information in dispute, at the address and in the manner established with the person. The notice shall include all relevant information regarding the dispute that the agency has received from the consumer.

(B) Provision of other information from consumer. The consumer reporting agency shall promptly provide to the person who provided the information in dispute all relevant information regarding the dispute that is received by the agency from the consumer after the period referred to in subparagraph (A) and before the end of the period referred to in paragraph (1)(A).

(3) Determination that dispute is frivolous or irrelevant.

(A) In general. Notwithstanding paragraph (1), a consumer reporting agency may terminate a reinvestigation of information disputed by a consumer under that paragraph if the agency reasonably determines that the dispute by the consumer is frivolous or irrelevant, including by reason of a failure by a consumer to provide sufficient information to investigate the disputed information.

(B) Notice of determination. Upon making any determination in accordance with subparagraph (A) that a dispute is frivolous or irrelevant, a consumer reporting agency shall notify the consumer of such determination not later than 5 business days after making such determination, by mail or, if authorized by the consumer for that purpose, by any other means available to the agency.

(C) Contents of notice. A notice under subparagraph (B) shall include

    (i)   the reasons for the determination under subparagraph (A); and

    (ii)   identification of any information required to investigate the disputed information, which may consist of a standardized form describing the general nature of such information.

(4) Consideration of consumer information. In conducting any reinvestigation under paragraph (1) with respect to disputed information in the file of any consumer, the consumer reporting agency shall review and consider all relevant information submitted by the consumer in the period described in paragraph (1)(A) with respect to such disputed information.

(5) Treatment of inaccurate or unverifiable information.

(A) In general. If, after any reinvestigation under paragraph (1) of any information disputed by a consumer, an item of the information is found to be inaccurate or incomplete or cannot be verified, the consumer reporting agency shall promptly delete that item of information from the consumer's file or modify that item of information, as appropriate, based on the results of the reinvestigation.

(B) Requirements relating to reinsertion of previously deleted material.

(i) Certification of accuracy of information. If any information is deleted from a consumer's file pursuant to subparagraph (A), the information may not be reinserted in the file by the consumer reporting agency unless the person who furnishes the information certifies that the information is complete and accurate.

(ii)   Notice to consumer. If any information that has been deleted from a consumer's file pursuant to subparagraph (A) is reinserted in the file, the consumer reporting agency shall notify the consumer of the reinsertion in writing not later than 5 business days after the reinsertion or, if authorized by the consumer for that purpose, by any other means available to the agency.

(iii)   Additional information. As part of, or in addition to, the notice under clause (ii), a consumer reporting agency shall provide to a consumer in writing not later than 5 business days after the date of the reinsertion

(I) a statement that the disputed information has been reinserted;

(II) the business name and address of any furnisher of information contacted and the telephone number of such furnisher, if reasonably available, or of any furnisher of information that contacted the consumer reporting agency, in connection with the reinsertion of such information; and

(III) a notice that the consumer has the right to add a statement to the consumer's file disputing the accuracy or completeness of the disputed information.

C) Procedures to prevent reappearance. A consumer reporting agency shall maintain reasonable procedures designed to prevent the reappearance in a consumer's file, and in consumer reports on the consumer, of information that is deleted pursuant to this paragraph (other than information that is reinserted in accordance with subparagraph (B)(i)).

D) Automated reinvestigation system. Any consumer reporting agency that compiles and maintains files on consumers on a nationwide basis shall implement an automated system through which furnishers of information to that consumer reporting agency may report the results of a reinvestigation that finds incomplete or inaccurate information in a consumer's file to other such consumer reporting agencies.

(6) Notice of results of reinvestigation.

(A) In general. A consumer reporting agency shall provide written notice to a consumer of the results of a reinvestigation under this subsection not later than 5 business days after the completion of the reinvestigation, by mail or, if authorized by the consumer for that purpose, by other means available to the agency.

(B) Contents. As part of, or in addition to, the notice

under subparagraph (A), a consumer reporting agency shall provide to a consumer in writing before the expiration of the 5-day period referred to in subparagraph (A)

(i)   a statement that the reinvestigation is completed;

(ii)   a consumer report that is based upon the consumer's file as that file is revised as a result of the reinvestigation;

(iii)   a notice that, if requested by the consumer, a description of the procedure used to determine the accuracy and completeness of the information shall be provided to the consumer by the agency, including the business name and address of any furnisher of information contacted in connection with such information and the telephone number of such furnisher, if reasonably available;

(iv)   a notice that the consumer has the right to add a statement to the consumer's file disputing the accuracy or completeness of the information; and

(v)   a notice that the consumer has the right to request under subsection (d) that the consumer reporting agency furnish notifications under that subsection.

(6) Description of reinvestigation procedure. A consumer reporting agency shall provide to a consumer a

description referred to in paragraph (6)(B)(iii) by not later than 15 days after receiving a request from the consumer for that description.

(7) Expedited dispute resolution. If a dispute regarding an item of information in a consumer's file at a consumer reporting agency is resolved in accordance with paragraph (5)(A) by the deletion of the disputed information by not later than 3 business days after the date on which the agency receives notice of the dispute from the consumer in accordance with paragraph (1)(A), then the agency shall not be required to comply with paragraphs (2), (6), and (7) with respect to that dispute if the agency

(A) provides prompt notice of the deletion to the consumer by telephone;

(B) includes in that notice, or in a written notice that accompanies a confirmation and consumer report provided in accordance with subparagraph (C), a statement of the consumer's right to request under subsection (d) that the agency furnish notifications under that subsection; and

(C) provides written confirmation of the deletion and a copy of a consumer report on the consumer that is based on the consumer's file after the deletion, not later than 5 business days after making the deletion.

(b) Statement of dispute. If the reinvestigation does not

resolve the dispute, the consumer may file a brief statement setting forth the nature of the dispute. The consumer reporting agency may limit such statements to not more than one hundred words if it provides the consumer with assistance in writing a clear summary of the dispute.

(c) Notification of consumer dispute in subsequent consumer reports. Whenever a statement of a dispute is filed, unless there is reasonable grounds to believe that it is frivolous or irrelevant, the consumer reporting agency shall, in any subsequent consumer report containing the information in question, clearly note that it is disputed by the consumer and provide either the consumer's statement or a clear and accurate codification or summary thereof.

(d) Notification of deletion of disputed information. Following any deletion of information which is found to be inaccurate or whose accuracy can no longer be verified or any notation as to disputed information, the consumer reporting agency shall, at the request of the consumer, furnish notification that the item has been deleted or the statement, codification or summary pursuant to subsection (b) or (c) of this section to any person specifically designated by the consumer who has within two years prior thereto received a consumer report for employment purposes, or within six months prior thereto received a consumer report for any other purpose, which contained the deleted or disputed information.

§ 612. Charges for certain disclosures [15 U.S.C. § 1681j]

(a) Reasonable charges allowed for certain disclosures.

(1) In general. Except as provided in subsections (b), (c), and (d), a consumer reporting agency may impose a reasonable charge on a consumer

(A) for making a disclosure to the consumer pursuant to section 609 [§1681g], which charge

(i) shall not exceed $8;(3) and

(ii) shall be indicated to the consumer before making the disclosure; and

(B) for furnishing, pursuant to 611(d) [§ 1681i], following a reinvestigation under section 611(a) [§ 1681i], a statement, codification, or summary to a person designated by the consumer under that section after the 30-day period beginning on the date of notification of the consumer under paragraph (6) or (8) of section 611(a) [§ 1681i] with respect to the reinvestigation, which charge

(i) shall not exceed the charge that the agency would impose on each designated recipient for a consumer report; and

(ii)   shall be indicated to the consumer before furnishing such information.

(2) Modification of amount. The Federal Trade Commission shall increase the amount referred to in paragraph (1)(A)(I) on January 1 of each year, based proportionally on changes in the Consumer Price Index, with fractional changes rounded to the nearest fifty cents.

(b) Free disclosure after adverse notice to consumer. Each consumer reporting agency that maintains a file on a consumer shall make all disclosures pursuant to section 609 [§ 1681g] without charge to the consumer if, not later than 60 days after receipt by such consumer of a notification pursuant to section 615 [§ 1681m], or of a notification from a debt collection agency affiliated with that consumer reporting agency stating that the consumer's credit rating may be or has been adversely affected, the consumer makes a request under section 609 [§ 1681g].

(c) Free disclosure under certain other circumstances. Upon the request of the consumer, a consumer reporting agency shall make all disclosures pursuant to section 609 [§ 1681g] once during any 12-month period without charge to that consumer if the consumer certifies in writing that the consumer

(1) is unemployed and intends to apply for employment in the 60-day period beginning on the date on which the certification is made;

(2) is a recipient of public welfare assistance; or

(2) has reason to believe that the file on the consumer at the agency contains inaccurate information due to fraud.

(d) Other charges prohibited. A consumer reporting agency shall not impose any charge on a consumer for providing any notification required by this title or making any disclosure required by this title, except as authorized by subsection (a).

§ 613. Public record information for employment purposes [15 U.S.C. §1681k]

(a) In general. A consumer reporting agency which furnishes a consumer report for employment purposes and which for that purpose compiles and reports items of information on consumers which are matters of public record and are likely to have an adverse effect upon a consumer's ability to obtain employment shall

(1) at the time such public record information is reported to the user of such consumer report, notify the consumer of the fact that public record information is being reported by the consumer reporting agency, together with the name and address of the person to whom such information is being reported; or

(2) maintain strict procedures designed to insure that whenever public record information which is likely to have an adverse effect on a consumer's ability to obtain employment is reported it is complete and up to date. For purposes of this paragraph, items of public record relating to arrests, indictments, convictions, suits, tax liens, and outstanding judgments shall be considered up to date if the current public record status of the item at the time of the report is reported.

(b) Exemption for national security investigations. Subsection (a) does not apply in the case of an agency or department of the United States Government that seeks to obtain and use a consumer report for employment purposes, if the head of the agency or department makes a written finding as prescribed under section 604(b)(4)(A).

§ 614. Restrictions on investigative consumer reports [15 U.S.C. § 1681l]

Whenever a consumer reporting agency prepares an investigative consumer report, no adverse information in the consumer report (other than information which is a matter of public record) may be included in a subsequent consumer report unless such adverse information has been verified in the process of making such subsequent consumer report, or the adverse information was received within the three-month period preceding the date the subsequent report is furnished.

§ 615. Requirements on users of consumer reports [15 U.S.C. § 1681m]

(a) Duties of users taking adverse actions on the basis of information contained in consumer reports. If any person takes any adverse action with respect to any consumer that is based in whole or in part on any information contained in a consumer report, the person shall

(1) provide oral, written, or electronic notice of the adverse action to the consumer;

(2) provide to the consumer orally, in writing, or electronically

(A) the name, address, and telephone number of the consumer reporting agency (including a toll-free telephone number established by the agency if the agency compiles and maintains files on consumers on a nationwide basis) that furnished the report to the person; and

(B) a statement that the consumer reporting agency did not make the decision to take the adverse action and is unable to provide the consumer the specific reasons why the adverse action was taken; and

(3) provide to the consumer an oral, written, or electronic notice of the consumer's right

(A) to obtain, under section 612 [§ 1681j], a free copy of a consumer report on the consumer from the consumer reporting agency referred to in paragraph (2), which notice shall include an indication of the 60-day period under that section for obtaining such a copy; and

(B) to dispute, under section 611 [§ 1681i], with a consumer reporting agency the accuracy or completeness of any information in a consumer report furnished by the agency.

(b) Adverse action based on information obtained from third parties other than consumer reporting agencies.

(1) In general. Whenever credit for personal, family, or household purposes involving a consumer is denied or the charge for such credit is increased either wholly or partly because of information obtained from a person other than a consumer reporting agency bearing upon the consumer's credit worthiness, credit standing, credit capacity, character, general reputation, personal characteristics, or mode of living, the user of such information shall, within a reasonable period of time, upon the consumer's written request for the reasons for such adverse action received within sixty days after learning of such adverse action, disclose the nature of the information to the consumer. The user of such information shall clearly and accurately disclose to the consumer his

right to make such written request at the time such adverse action is communicated to the consumer.

(2) Duties of person taking certain actions based on information provided by affiliate.

(A) Duties, generally. If a person takes an action described in subparagraph (B) with respect to a consumer, based in whole or in part on information described in subparagraph (C), the person shall

(i)　notify the consumer of the action, including a statement that the consumer may obtain the information in accordance with clause (ii); and

(ii)　upon a written request from the consumer received within 60 days after transmittal of the notice required by clause (I), disclose to the consumer the nature of the information upon which the action is based by not later than 30 days after receipt of the request.

(B) Action described. An action referred to in subparagraph (A) is an adverse action described in section 603(k)(1)(A) [§ 1681a], taken in connection with a transaction initiated by the consumer, or any adverse action described in clause (i) or (ii) of section 603(k)(1)(B) [§ 1681a].

(C) Information described. Information referred to in subparagraph (A)

(i) except as provided in clause (ii), is information that

(I) is furnished to the person taking the action by a person related by common ownership or affiliated by common corporate control to the person taking the action; and

(II) bears on the credit worthiness, credit standing, credit, capacity, character, general reputation, personal characteristics, or mode of living of the consumer; and

(ii) does not include

(I) information solely as to transactions or experiences between the consumer and the person furnishing the information; or

(II) information in a consumer report.

(c) Reasonable procedures to assure compliance. No person shall be held liable for any violation of this section if he shows by a preponderance of the evidence that at the time of the alleged violation he maintained reasonable procedures to assure compliance with the provisions of this section.

(d) Duties of users making written credit or insurance solicitations on the basis of information contained in consumer files.

(1) In general. Any person who uses a consumer report on any consumer in connection with any credit or insurance transaction that is not initiated by the consumer, that is provided to that person under section 604(c)(1)(B) [§ 1681b], shall provide with each written solicitation made to the consumer regarding the transaction a clear and conspicuous statement that

(A) information contained in the consumer's consumer report was used in connection with the transaction;

(B) the consumer received the offer of credit or insurance because the consumer satisfied the criteria for credit worthiness or insurability under which the consumer was selected for the offer;

(C) if applicable, the credit or insurance may not be extended if, after the consumer responds to the offer, the consumer does not meet the criteria used to select the consumer for the offer or any applicable criteria bearing on credit worthiness or insurability or does not furnish any required collateral;

(D) the consumer has a right to prohibit information

contained in the consumer's file with any consumer reporting agency from being used in connection with any credit or insurance transaction that is not initiated by the consumer; and

(E) the consumer may exercise the right referred to in subparagraph (D) by notifying a notification system established under section 604(e) [§ 1681b].

(2) Disclosure of address and telephone number. A statement under paragraph (1) shall include the address and toll-free telephone number of the appropriate notification system established under section 604(e) [§1681b].

(3) Maintaining criteria on file. A person who makes an offer of credit or insurance to a consumer under a credit or insurance transaction described in paragraph (1) shall maintain on file the criteria used to select the consumer to receive the offer, all criteria bearing on credit worthiness or insurability, as applicable, that are the basis for determining whether or not to extend credit or insurance pursuant to the offer, and any requirement for the furnishing of collateral as a condition of the extension of credit or insurance, until the expiration of the 3-year period beginning on the date on which the offer is made to the consumer.

(4) Authority of federal agencies regarding unfair or deceptive acts or practices not affected. This section is not intended to affect the authority of any Federal or

State agency to enforce a prohibition against unfair or deceptive acts or practices, including the making of false or misleading statements in connection with a credit or insurance transaction that is not initiated by the consumer.

§ 616. Civil liability for willful noncompliance [15 U.S.C. § 1681n]

(a) In general. Any person who willfully fails to comply with any requirement imposed under this title with respect to any consumer is liable to that consumer in an amount equal to the sum of

(1)(A) any actual damages sustained by the consumer as a result of the failure or damages of not less than $100 and not more than $1,000; or

(B) in the case of liability of a natural person for obtaining a consumer report under false pretenses or knowingly without a permissible purpose, actual damages sustained by the consumer as a result of the failure or $1,000, whichever is greater;

(2) such amount of punitive damages as the court may allow; and

(3) in the case of any successful action to enforce any liability under this section, the costs of the action together with reasonable attorney's fees as determined by the court.

(b) Civil liability for knowing noncompliance. Any person who obtains a consumer report from a consumer reporting agency under false pretenses or knowingly without a permissible purpose shall be liable to the consumer reporting agency for actual damages sustained by the consumer reporting agency or $1,000, whichever is greater.

(c) Attorney's fees. Upon a finding by the court that an unsuccessful pleading, motion, or other paper filed in connection with an action under this section was filed in bad faith or for purposes of harassment, the court shall award to the prevailing party attorney's fees reasonable in relation to the work expended in responding to the pleading, motion, or other paper.

§ 617. Civil liability for negligent noncompliance [15 U.S.C. § 1681o]

(a) In general. Any person who is negligent in failing to comply with any requirement imposed under this title with respect to any consumer is liable to that consumer in an amount equal to the sum of

(1) any actual damages sustained by the consumer as a result of the failure;

(2) in the case of any successful action to enforce any liability under this section, the costs of the action together with reasonable attorney's fees as determined by the court.

(c) Attorney's fees. On a finding by the court that an unsuccessful pleading, motion, or other paper filed in connection with an action under this section was filed in bad faith or for purposes of harassment, the court shall award to the prevailing party attorney's fees reasonable in relation to the work expended in responding to the pleading, motion, or other paper.

§ 618. Jurisdiction of courts; limitation of actions [15 U.S.C. § 1681p] An action to enforce any liability created under this title may be brought in any appropriate United States district court without regard to the amount in controversy, or in any other court of competent jurisdiction, within two years from the date on which the liability arises, except that where a defendant has materially and willfully misrepresented any information required under this title to be disclosed to an individual and the information so misrepresented is material to the establishment of the defendant's liability to that individual under this title, the action may be brought at any time within two years after discovery by the individual of the misrepresentation.

§ 619. Obtaining information under false pretenses [15 U.S.C. § 1681q] Any person who knowingly and willfully obtains information on a consumer from a consumer reporting agency under false pretenses shall be fined under title 18, United States Code, imprisoned for not more than 2 years, or both.

§ 620. Unauthorized disclosures by officers or employees [15 U.S.C. §1681r] Any officer or employee of a consumer reporting agency who knowingly and willfully provides information concerning an individual from the agency's files to a person not authorized to receive that information shall be fined under title 18, United States Code, imprisoned for not more than 2 years, or both.

§ 621. Administrative enforcement [15 U.S.C. § 1681s]

(a) (1) Enforcement by Federal Trade Commission. Compliance with the requirements imposed under this title shall be enforced under the Federal Trade Commission Act [15 U.S.C. §§ 41 et seq.] by the Federal Trade Commission with respect to consumer reporting agencies and all other persons subject thereto, except to the extent that enforcement of the requirements imposed under this title is specifically committed to some other government agency under subsection (b) hereof. For the purpose of the exercise by the Federal Trade Commission of its functions and powers under the Federal Trade Commission Act, a violation of any requirement or prohibition imposed under this title shall constitute an unfair or deceptive act or practice in commerce in violation of section 5(a) of the Federal Trade Commission Act [15 U.S.C. § 45(a)] and shall be subject to enforcement by the Federal Trade Commission under section 5(b) thereof [15 U.S.C. § 45(b)] with respect to any consumer reporting agency or person subject to enforcement by the Federal Trade Commission pursuant to this subsection, irrespective of whether that person is engaged in commerce or meets any other jurisdictional tests in the Federal Trade Commission Act. The Federal Trade Commission shall have such procedural, investigative, and enforcement powers, including the power to issue procedural rules in enforcing compliance with the requirements imposed under this title and to require the filing of reports, the production of documents, and the appearance of witnesses as though the applicable terms and conditions of the Federal Trade Commission Act were part of this title. Any person violating any of the provisions of this title shall be subject to the penalties and entitled to the privileges and immunities provided in the Federal Trade Commission Act as though the applicable terms and provisions thereof were part of this title.

(2)(A) In the event of a knowing violation, which constitutes a pattern or practice of violations of this title, the Commission may commence a civil action to recover a civil penalty in a district court of the United States against any person that violates this title. In such action, such person shall be liable for a civil penalty of not more than $2,500 per violation.

(B) In determining the amount of a civil penalty under subparagraph (A), the court shall take into account the degree of culpability, any history of prior such conduct, ability to pay, effect on ability to continue to do business, and such other matters as justice may require.

(3) Notwithstanding paragraph (2), a court may not

impose any civil penalty on a person for a violation of section 623(a)(1) [§ 1681s-2] unless the person has been enjoined from committing the violation, or ordered not to commit the violation, in an action or proceeding brought by or on behalf of the Federal Trade Commission, and has violated the injunction or order, and the court may not impose any civil penalty for any violation occurring before the date of the violation of the injunction or order.

(b) Enforcement by other agencies. Compliance with the requirements imposed under this title with respect to consumer reporting agencies, persons who use consumer reports from such agencies, persons who furnish information to such agencies, and users of information that are subject to subsection (d) of section 615 [§ 1681m] shall be enforced under

(1) section 8 of the Federal Deposit Insurance Act [12 U.S.C. § 1818], in the case of

(A) national banks, and Federal branches and Federal agencies of foreign banks, by the Office of the Comptroller of the Currency;

(B) member banks of the Federal Reserve System (other than national banks), branches and agencies of foreign banks (other than Federal branches, Federal agencies, and insured State branches of foreign banks), commercial lending companies owned or controlled by foreign banks, and organizations operating under section 25 or 25(a) [25A] of the

Federal Reserve Act [12 U.S.C. §§ 601 et seq., §§ 611 et seq], by the Board of Governors of the Federal Reserve System; and

(C) banks insured by the Federal Deposit Insurance Corporation (other than members of the Federal Reserve System) and insured State branches of foreign banks, by the Board of Directors of the Federal Deposit Insurance Corporation;

(2) section 8 of the Federal Deposit Insurance Act [12 U.S.C. § 1818], by the Director of the Office of Thrift Supervision, in the case of a savings association the deposits of which are insured by the Federal Deposit Insurance Corporation;

(3) the Federal Credit Union Act [12 U.S.C. §§ 1751 et seq.], by the Administrator of the National Credit Union Administration [National Credit Union Administration Board] with respect to any Federal credit union;

(4) subtitle IV of title 49 [49 U.S.C. §§ 10101 et seq.], by the Secretary of Transportation, with respect to all carriers subject to the jurisdiction of the Surface Transportation Board;

(5) the Federal Aviation Act of 1958 [49 U.S.C. Appx §§ 1301 et seq.], by the Secretary of Transportation with respect to any air carrier or foreign air carrier subject to that Act [49 U.S.C. Appx §§ 1301 et seq.]; and

(6) the Packers and Stockyards Act, 1921 [7 U.S.C. §§ 181 et seq.] (except as provided in section 406 of that Act [7 U.S.C. §§ 226 and 227]), by the Secretary of Agriculture with respect to any activities subject to that Act.

The terms used in paragraph (1) that are not defined in this title or otherwise defined in section 3(s) of the Federal Deposit Insurance Act (12 U.S.C. §1813(s)) shall have the meaning given to them in section 1(b) of the International Banking Act of 1978 (12 U.S.C. § 3101).

(d) State action for violations.

(1) Authority of states. In addition to such other remedies as are provided under State law, if the chief law enforcement officer of a State, or an official or agency designated by a State, has reason to believe that any person has violated or is violating this title, the State

(A) may bring an action to enjoin such violation in any appropriate United States district court or in any other court of competent jurisdiction;

(B) subject to paragraph (5), may bring an action on behalf of the residents of the State to recover

(i)   damages for which the person is liable to such residents under sections 616 and 617 [§§ 1681n and 1681o] as a result of the violation;

    (ii)   in the case of a violation of section 623(a) [§ 1681s-2], damages for which the person would, but for section 623(c) [§1681s-2], be liable to such residents as a result of the violation; or

    (iii)   damages of not more than $1,000 for each willful or negligent violation; and

(C) in the case of any successful action subparagraph (A) or (B), shall be awarded the costs of the action and reasonable attorney fees as determined by the court.

(2) Rights of federal regulators. The State shall serve prior written notice of any action under paragraph (1) upon the Federal Trade Commission or the appropriate Federal regulator determined under subsection (b) and provide the Commission or appropriate Federal regulator with a copy of its complaint, except in any case in which such prior notice is not feasible, in which case the State shall serve such notice immediately upon instituting such action. The Federal Trade Commission or appropriate Federal regulator shall have the right

(A) to intervene in the action;

(B) upon so intervening, to be heard on all matters arising

therein;

(C) to remove the action to the appropriate United States district court; and

(D) to file petitions for appeal.

(3) Investigatory powers. For purposes of bringing any action under this subsection, nothing in this subsection shall prevent the chief law enforcement officer, or an official or agency designated by a State, from exercising the powers conferred on the chief law enforcement officer or such official by the laws of such State to conduct investigations or to administer oaths or affirmations or to compel the attendance of witnesses or the production of documentary and other evidence.

(4) Limitation on state action while federal action pending. If the Federal Trade Commission or the appropriate Federal regulator has instituted a civil action or an administrative action under section 8 of the Federal Deposit Insurance Act for a violation of this title, no State may, during the pendency of such action, bring an action under this section against any defendant named in the complaint of the Commission or the appropriate Federal regulator for any violation of this title that is alleged in that complaint.

(5) Limitations on state actions for violation of section 623(a)(1) [§1681s-2].

(A) Violation of injunction required. A State may not bring an action against a person under paragraph (1)(B) for a violation of section 623(a)(1) [§ 1681s-2], unless

(i) the person has been enjoined from committing the violation, in an action brought by the State under paragraph (1)(A); and

(ii) the person has violated the injunction.

(B) Limitation on damages recoverable. In an action against a person under paragraph (1)(B) for a violation of section 623(a)(1) [§1681s-2], a State may not recover any damages incurred before the date of the violation of an injunction on which the action is based.

(d) Enforcement under other authority. For the purpose of the exercise by any agency referred to in subsection (b) of this section of its powers under any Act referred to in that subsection, a violation of any requirement imposed under this title shall be deemed to be a violation of a requirement imposed under that Act. In addition to its powers under any provision of law specifically referred to in subsection (b) of this section, each of the agencies referred to in that subsection may exercise, for the purpose of enforcing compliance with any requirement imposed under this title any other authority conferred on it by law.

(e) Regulatory authority

(1) The Federal banking agencies referred to in paragraphs (1) and (2) of subsection (b) shall jointly prescribe such regulations as necessary to carry out the purposes of this Act with respect to any persons identified under paragraphs (1) and (2) of subsection (b), and the Board of Governors of the Federal Reserve System shall have authority to prescribe regulations consistent with such joint regulations with respect to bank holding companies and affiliates (other than depository institutions and consumer reporting agencies) of such holding companies.

(2) The Board of the National Credit Union Administration shall prescribe such regulations as necessary to carry out the purposes of this Act with respect to any persons identified under paragraph (3) of subsection (b).

§ 622. Information on overdue child support obligations [15 U.S.C. §1681s-1] Notwithstanding any other provision of this title, a consumer reporting agency shall include in any consumer report furnished by the agency in accordance with section 604 [§ 1681b] of this title, any information on the failure of the consumer to pay overdue support which

(1) is provided

(A) to the consumer reporting agency by a State or local child support enforcement agency; or

(B) to the consumer reporting agency and verified by any local, State, or Federal government agency; and

(2) antedates the report by 7 years or less.

§ 623. Responsibilities of furnishers of information to consumer reporting agencies [15 U.S.C. § 1681s-2]

(a) Duty of furnishers of information to provide accurate information.

(1) Prohibition.

(A) Reporting information with actual knowledge of errors. A person shall not furnish any information relating to a consumer to any consumer reporting agency if the person knows or consciously avoids knowing that the information is inaccurate.

(B) Reporting information after notice and confirmation of errors. A person shall not furnish information relating to a consumer to any consumer reporting agency if

(i)   the person has been notified by the consumer, at the address specified by the person for such notices, that specific information is inaccurate; and

(ii)   the information is, in fact, inaccurate.

(C) No address requirement. A person who clearly and conspicuously specifies to the consumer an address for notices referred to in subparagraph (B) shall not be subject to subparagraph (A); however, nothing in subparagraph (B) shall require a person to specify such an address.

(2) Duty to correct and update information. A person who

(A) regularly and in the ordinary course of business furnishes information to one or more consumer reporting agencies about the person's transactions or experiences with any consumer; and

(B) has furnished to a consumer reporting agency information that the person determines is not complete or accurate, shall promptly notify the consumer reporting agency of that determination and provide to the agency any corrections to that information, or any additional information, that is necessary to make the information provided by the person to the agency complete and accurate, and shall not thereafter furnish to the agency any of the information that remains not complete or accurate.

(3) Duty to provide notice of dispute. If the completeness or accuracy of any information furnished by any person to any consumer reporting agency is disputed to such person by a consumer, the person may not furnish the information to any consumer reporting agency

without notice that such information is disputed by the consumer.

(4) Duty to provide notice of closed accounts. A person who regularly and in the ordinary course of business furnishes information to a consumer reporting agency regarding a consumer who has a credit account with that person shall notify the agency of the voluntary closure of the account by the consumer, in information regularly furnished for the period in which the account is closed.

(5) Duty to provide notice of delinquency of accounts. A person who furnishes information to a consumer reporting agency regarding a delinquent account being placed for collection, charged to profit or loss, or subjected to any similar action shall, not later than 90 days after furnishing the information, notify the agency of the month and year of the commencement of the delinquency that immediately preceded the action.

(b) Duties of furnishers of information upon notice of dispute.

(1) In general. After receiving notice pursuant to section 611(a)(2) [§1681i] of a dispute with regard to the completeness or accuracy of any information provided by a person to a consumer reporting agency, the person shall

(A) conduct an investigation with respect to the disputed

information;

(B) review all relevant information provided by the consumer reporting agency pursuant to section 611(a)(2) [§ 1681i];

(C) report the results of the investigation to the consumer reporting agency; and

(D) if the investigation finds that the information is incomplete or inaccurate, report those results to all other consumer reporting agencies to which the person furnished the information and that compile and maintain files on consumers on a nationwide basis.

(2) Deadline. A person shall complete all investigations, reviews, and reports required under paragraph (1) regarding information provided by the person to a consumer reporting agency, before the expiration of the period under section 611(a)(1) [§ 1681i] within which the consumer reporting agency is required to complete actions required by that section regarding that information.

(d) Limitation on liability. Sections 616 and 617 [§§ 1681n and 1681o] do not apply to any failure to comply with subsection (a), except as provided in section 621(c)(1)(B) [§ 1681s].

(e) Limitation on enforcement. Subsection (a) shall be

enforced exclusively under section 621 [§ 1681s] by the Federal agencies and officials and the State officials identified in that section.

§ 624. Relation to State laws [15 U.S.C. § 1681t]

(a) In general. Except as provided in subsections (b) and (c), this title does not annul, alter, affect, or exempt any person subject to the provisions of this title from complying with the laws of any State with respect to the collection, distribution, or use of any information on consumers, except to the extent that those laws are inconsistent with any provision of this title, and then only to the extent of the inconsistency.

(b) General exceptions. No requirement or prohibition may be imposed under the laws of any State

(1) with respect to any subject matter regulated under

(A) subsection (c) or (e) of section 604 [§ 1681b], relating to the prescreening of consumer reports;

(B) section 611 [§ 1681i], relating to the time by which a consumer reporting agency must take any action, including the provision of notification to a consumer or other person, in any procedure related to the disputed accuracy of information in a consumer's file, except that this subparagraph shall not apply to any State law in effect on the date of enactment of the Consumer Credit Reporting Reform Act of 1996;

(C) subsections (a) and (b) of section 615 [§ 1681m], relating to the duties of a person who takes any adverse action with respect to a consumer;

(D) section 615(d) [§ 1681m], relating to the duties of persons who use a consumer report of a consumer in connection with any credit or insurance transaction that is not initiated by the consumer and that consists of a firm offer of credit or insurance;

(E) section 605 [§ 1681c], relating to information contained in consumer reports, except that this subparagraph shall not apply to any State law in effect on the date of enactment of the Consumer Credit Reporting Reform Act of 1996; or

(F) section 623 [§ 1681s-2], relating to the responsibilities of persons who furnish information to consumer reporting agencies, except that this paragraph shall not apply

    (i)   with respect to section 54A(a) of chapter 93 of the Massachusetts Annotated Laws (as in effect on the date of enactment of the Consumer Credit Reporting Reform Act of 1996); or

    (ii)   with respect to section 1785.25(a) of the California Civil Code (as in effect on the date of enactment of the Consumer Credit Reporting Reform Act of 1996);

(2) with respect to the exchange of information among

persons affiliated by common ownership or common corporate control, except that this paragraph shall not apply with respect to subsection (a) or (c)(1) of section 2480e of title 9, Vermont Statutes Annotated (as in effect on the date of enactment of the Consumer Credit Reporting Reform Act of 1996); or

(3) with respect to the form and content of any disclosure required to be made under section 609(c) [§ 1681g].

(c) Definition of firm offer of credit or insurance. Notwithstanding any definition of the term "firm offer of credit or insurance" (or any equivalent term) under the laws of any State, the definition of that term contained in section 603(l) [§ 1681a] shall be construed to apply in the enforcement and interpretation of the laws of any State governing consumer reports.

(d) Limitations. Subsections (b) and (c)

(1) do not affect any settlement, agreement, or consent judgment between any State Attorney General and any consumer reporting agency in effect on the date of enactment of the Consumer Credit Reporting Reform Act of 1996; and

(2) do not apply to any provision of State law (including any provision of a State constitution) that

(A) is enacted after January 1, 2004;

(B) states explicitly that the provision is intended to supplement this title; and

(C) gives greater protection to consumers than is provided under this title.

§ 625. Disclosures to FBI for counterintelligence purposes [15 U.S.C. §1681u]

(a) Identity of financial institutions. Notwithstanding section 604 [§1681b] or any other provision of this title, a consumer reporting agency shall furnish to the Federal Bureau of Investigation the names and addresses of all financial institutions (as that term is defined in section 1101 of the Right to Financial Privacy Act of 1978 [12 U.S.C. §3401]) at which a consumer maintains or has maintained an account, to the extent that information is in the files of the agency, when presented with a written request for that information, signed by the Director of the Federal Bureau of Investigation, or the Director's designee in a position not lower than Deputy Assistant Director at Bureau headquarters or a Special Agent in Charge of a Bureau field office designated by the Director, which certifies compliance with this section. The Director or the Director's designee may make such a certification only if the Director or the Director's designee has determined in writing, that such information is sought for the conduct of an authorized investigation to protect against international terrorism or clandestine intelligence activities, provided that such an investigation of a United States person is not conducted solely upon the basis of activities protected by the first amendment to the Constitution of the United States.

(b) Identifying information. Notwithstanding the provisions of section 604 [§1681b] or any other provision of this title, a consumer reporting agency shall furnish identifying information respecting a consumer, limited to name, address, former addresses, places of employment, or former places of employment, to the Federal Bureau of Investigation when presented with a written request, signed by the Director or the Director's designee, which certifies compliance with this subsection. The Director or the Director's designee in a position not lower than Deputy Assistant Director at Bureau headquarters or a Special Agent in Charge of a Bureau field office designated by the Director may make such a certification only if the Director or the Director's designee has determined in writing that such information is sought for the conduct of an authorized investigation to protect against international terrorism or clandestine intelligence activities, provided that such an investigation of a United States person is not conducted solely upon the basis of activities protected by the first amendment to the Constitution of the United States.

(c) Court order for disclosure of consumer reports. Notwithstanding section 604 [§ 1681b] or any other provision of this title, if requested in writing by the Director of the Federal Bureau of Investigation, or a designee of the Director in a position not lower than Deputy Assistant Director at Bureau headquarters or a

Special Agent in Charge of a Bureau field office designated by the Director, a court may issue an order ex parte directing a consumer reporting agency to furnish a consumer report to the Federal Bureau of Investigation, upon a showing in camera that the consumer report is sought for the conduct of an authorized investigation to protect against international terrorism or clandestine intelligence activities, provided that such an investigation of a United States person is not conducted solely upon the basis of activities protected by the first amendment to the Constitution of the United States. The terms of an order issued under this subsection shall not disclose that the order is issued for purposes of a counterintelligence investigation.

(d) Confidentiality. No consumer reporting agency or officer, employee, or agent of a consumer reporting agency shall disclose to any person, other than those officers, employees, or agents of a consumer reporting agency necessary to fulfill the requirement to disclose information to the Federal Bureau of Investigation under this section, that the Federal Bureau of Investigation has sought or obtained the identity of financial institutions or a consumer report respecting any consumer under subsection (a), (b), or (c), and no consumer reporting agency or officer, employee, or agent of a consumer reporting agency shall include in any consumer report any information that would indicate that the Federal Bureau of Investigation has sought or obtained such information or a consumer report.

(e) Payment of fees. The Federal Bureau of Investigation shall, subject to the availability of appropriations, pay to the consumer reporting agency assembling or providing report or information in accordance with procedures established under this section a fee for reimbursement for such costs as are reasonably necessary and which have been directly incurred in searching, reproducing, or transporting books, papers, records, or other data required or requested to be produced under this section.

(f) Limit on dissemination. The Federal Bureau of Investigation may not disseminate information obtained pursuant to this section outside of the Federal Bureau of Investigation, except to other Federal agencies as may be necessary for the approval or conduct of a foreign counterintelligence investigation, or, where the information concerns a person subject to the Uniform Code of Military Justice, to appropriate investigative authorities within the military department concerned as may be necessary for the conduct of a joint foreign counterintelligence investigation.

(g) Rules of construction. Nothing in this section shall be construed to prohibit information from being furnished by the Federal Bureau of Investigation pursuant to a subpoena or court order, in connection with a judicial or administrative proceeding to enforce the provisions of this Act. Nothing in this section shall be construed to authorize or permit the withholding of information from the Congress.

(h) Reports to Congress. On a semiannual basis, the Attorney General shall fully inform the Permanent Select Committee on Intelligence and the Committee on Banking, Finance and Urban Affairs of the House of Representatives, and the Select Committee on Intelligence and the Committee on Banking, Housing, and Urban Affairs of the Senate concerning all requests made pursuant to subsections (a), (b), and (c).

(i)   Damages. Any agency or department of the United States obtaining or disclosing any consumer reports, records, or information contained therein in violation of this section is liable to the consumer to whom such consumer reports, records, or information relate in an amount equal to the sum of

(1) $100, without regard to the volume of consumer reports, records, or information involved;

(2) any actual damages sustained by the consumer as a result of the disclosure;

(3) if the violation is found to have been willful or intentional, such punitive damages as a court may allow; and

(4) in the case of any successful action to enforce liability under this subsection, the costs of the action, together with reasonable attorney fees, as determined by the court.

(j) Disciplinary actions for violations. If a court determines that any agency or department of the United States has violated any provision of this section and the court finds that the circumstances surrounding the violation raise questions of whether or not an officer or employee of the agency or department acted willfully or intentionally with respect to the violation, the agency or department shall promptly initiate a proceeding to determine whether or not disciplinary action is warranted against the officer or employee who was responsible for the violation.

(k) Good-faith exception. Notwithstanding any other provision of this title, any consumer reporting agency or agent or employee thereof making disclosure of consumer reports or identifying information pursuant to this subsection in good-faith reliance upon a certification of the Federal Bureau of Investigation pursuant to provisions of this section shall not be liable to any person for such disclosure under this title, the constitution of any State, or any law or regulation of any State or any political subdivision of any State.

(l) Limitation of remedies. Notwithstanding any other provision of this title, the remedies and sanctions set forth in this section shall be the only judicial remedies and sanctions for violation of this section.

(m) Injunctive relief. In addition to any other remedy contained in this section, injunctive relief shall be available to require compliance with the procedures of this section. In the event of any successful action under this subsection, costs together with reasonable attorney fees, as determined by the court, may be recovered.

§ 626. Disclosures to governmental agencies for counterterrorism purposes [15 U.S.C. §1681v]

(a) Disclosure. Notwithstanding section 604 or any other provision of this title, a consumer reporting agency shall furnish a consumer report of a consumer and all other information in a consumer's file to a government agency authorized to conduct investigations of, or intelligence or counterintelligence activities or analysis related to, international terrorism when presented with a written certification by such government agency that such information is necessary for the agency's conduct or such investigation, activity or analysis.

(b) Form of certification. The certification described in subsection (a) shall be signed by a supervisory official designated by the head of a Federal agency or an officer of a Federal agency whose appointment to office is required to be made by the President, by and with the advice and consent of the Senate.

(c) Confidentiality. No consumer reporting agency, or officer, employee, or agent of such consumer reporting agency, shall disclose to any person, or specify in any consumer report, that a government agency has sought or obtained access to information under subsection (a).

(d) Rule of construction. Nothing in section 625 shall be

construed to limit the authority of the Director of the Federal Bureau of Investigation under this section.

(e) Safe harbor. Notwithstanding any other provision of this title, any consumer reporting agency or agent or employee thereof making disclosure of consumer reports or other information pursuant to this section in good-faith reliance upon a certification of a governmental agency pursuant to the provisions of this section shall not be liable to any person for such disclosure under this subchapter, the constitution of any State, or any law or regulation of any State or any political subdivision of any State.

Legislative History
House Reports:
No. 91-975 (Comm. on Banking and Currency) and
No. 91-1587 (Comm. of Conference)

Senate Reports:
No. 91-1139 accompanying S. 3678 (Comm. on Banking and Currency)

Congressional Record, Vol. 116 (1970)
May 25, considered and passed House.
Sept. 18, considered and passed Senate, amended.
Oct. 9, Senate agreed to conference report.
Oct. 13, House agreed to conference report.

Enactment:

Public Law No. 91-508 (October 26, 1970):

Amendments: Public Law Nos.
95-473 (October 17, 1978)
95-598 (November 6, 1978)
98-443 (October 4, 1984)
101-73 (August 9, 1989)
102-242 (December 19, 1991)
102-537 (October 27, 1992)
102-550 (October 28, 1992)
103-325 (September 23, 1994)
104-88 (December 29, 1995)
104-93 (January 6, 1996)
104-193 (August 22, 1996)
104-208 (September 30, 1996)
105-107 (November 20, 1997)
105-347 (November 2, 1998)
106-102 (November 12, 1999)
107-56 (October 26, 2001)

Endnotes:
1. The reporting periods have been lengthened for certain adverse information pertaining to U.S. Government insured or guaranteed student loans, or pertaining to national direct student loans. See sections 430A(f) and 463(c)(3) of the Higher Education Act of 1965, 20 U.S.C. 1080a(f) and 20 U.S.C. 1087cc(c)(3), respectively.

2. Should read "paragraphs (4) and (5)...." Prior Section 605(a)(6) was amended and re-designated as Section 605(a)(5) in November 1998.

3. The Federal Trade Commission increased the maximum allowable charge to $9.00, effective January 1, 2002. 66 Fed. Reg. 63545 (Dec. 7, 2001).

CHAPTER 9

FREQUENTLY ASKED CREDIT QUESTIONS & ANSWERS

1. What is credit scoring?

Credit scoring is a numeric number given to an individual by a credit-reporting agency. A credit score is a scientific method of determining your probability of paying bills on time. It is based on your credit history. It considers your number and type of credit accounts, your credit available, how much you owe, and your payment history.

Scores range from 375 to 900 points.

"Excellent credit" usually means that you have no significant late payments of 60 days or more on any types of credit in the past 3 years. Examples of excellent credit scores are 680 or better.

"Good credit" usually means you have no late payments on any loan for the previous two years. Good credit scores range from 620 to 680. In most cases, a score of 620 is the cutoff for better rates on mortgages, loans and credit cards. However, each and every creditor makes their own decisions and may consider other factors like your income, years at residence, work history and household income.

"Fair credit" usually indicates some 60 days or more late payments on credit obligations. Credit scores can range from 580-619. A score of 580 is often the cutoff for major mortgage loan companies to qualify for a mortgage. Bankruptcies must be clear and discharged for at least two years to qualify as fair credit, as needed to qualify for a mortgage approval through Fannie Mae and Freddie Mac.

"Poor credit" involves many significant "60 days" or later payments. "Poor credit" is scores below 580.

2. What are "inquiries" on my credit report?

Inquiries are indicated on your credit report when you apply for credit and a creditor checks your credit report.

3. Why do "inquiries" hurt my credit score?

Many credit card and mortgage applications are rejected because of too many inquiries. This is because as you seek credit, you indicate that you are either careless or desperate. Also, inquiries indicate that you may be getting a lot of new credit obligations that you cannot afford to pay. Generally, more than 6 inquiries in 12 months on your report are considered too many.

4. I made late payments, but recently paid off those accounts. Is my credit now good?

Late payments hurt your credit even if you already paid your account off in full. After 12 months of full payments or on-time payments, your credit will improve significantly. It will take three full years to have good credit. Review question number 1 above about credit scoring to learn more. Your late payments remain on your credit report for 7 years. Late payments indicate that you are either lazy in paying your bills or not very good at managing your money.

5. What is the best way to improve my credit?

The best way to have good credit is to pay your bills on time. If you have bad credit, the best way to improve your credit report and credit score is to dispute your bad credit.

The Fair Credit Reporting Act requires credit bureaus to be precise and accurate. Also, dispute the debt with the creditor who reported it. The creditor is responsible for verifying consumer disputes. If you still owe money to the creditor, use the all-powerful negotiating tactic of "full debt settlement" in exchange for partial payment on the debt. Insist on a letter from the credit company to the credit bureaus that confirm you have paid your account in full and to remove any late remarks

on your report.

6. What is included on my credit report?

- Identifying information

- Employment information

- Credit information

- Public records like judgments

- Inquiries

7. What is not included on credit reports?

- Your religion

- Your health

- Your criminal past

- Your income

- Your race

- Your driving record

8. What are the 3 major credit bureaus?

Equifax 1-800-685-1111 www.equifax.com

Experian 1-888-397-3742 www.experian.com

Trans Union 1-800-916-8800 www.transunion.com

9. I have been refused credit. Can I do something about it?

Yes. Almost 90% of all people have a problem with their

credit reports. Frequently, credit reports are outdated or just

wrong. You can dispute wrong and outdated information. You

can even ask for verification of partially correct credit

problems. If the credit bureau does not verify the credit quickly, you can ask for the bad credit remark to be removed.

10. Is the credit bureau a part of the government?

No, credit bureaus are not government entities. They are public companies listed on the stock exchange.

11. Is it illegal to fix or clear up your credit?

It is legal to fix and clear up your credit. The government has passed special laws requiring the credit bureaus to fix and clear up any bad credit remarks they fail to verify, following your proper request.

12. How can I get a copy of my credit report?

Just call any or all of the 3 credit bureaus listed above (in question #8) and ask for a copy. If you have been denied credit based on the credit report, you are entitled to receive a free copy. Otherwise, you may pay $9.00 or $10.00 for a copy of each report.

13. How can I get a copy of my credit score?

All 3 credit bureaus keep a score on you. Just ask for your score from the credit bureau. They will ask you for a small payment for a copy of your credit score. When you receive your credit score report, it may include an explanation of what is affecting your rate, such as positive and negative contributing factors.

14. How often does my credit score change?

Your credit score will often change daily. The credit bureaus receive new information daily from your creditors. So, your score can change daily. However, only a major event, like not paying on time or new debt would have a major change on your score. So, your score should stay within ten points daily.

15. Do all 3 credit bureaus have the same credit information and same credit score?

No. The people who you owe money to do not have to report anything to the credit bureaus. Each credit card company and mortgage company have made separate agreements on when and how often to report your credit information.

16. Who can request my credit report?

Under the Fair Credit Reporting Act, your report is private and can only be released to the following:

- Anyone you give permission to review your credit;

- Your employer;

- Your insurance company to review an application for insurance;

- A review for eligibility for a license;

- A court order;

- An IRS subpoena.

CHAPTER 10

GREAT INTERNET SITES TO:

1. GET FREE CREDIT REPORTS
2. ASK YOUR CREDIT QUESTIONS
3. READ ABOUT HOW TO IMPROVE YOUR CREDIT & GET PRIME CREDIT CARDS

The internet has hundreds of millions of pages. A vast amount of great information is available about credit and credit repair.

My favorite sites include:

WWW.ARTOFCREDIT.COM

This interesting site is "a place where you can get the latest insider information" including information on how to get credit cards, business credit, and mortgages.

WWW.CREDITNET.COM

This internet site includes a library of credit card facts, emergency services, credit card offers, credit repair services, credit repair facts, do-it-yourself credit repair, and an outstanding discussion forum.

WWW.FTC.GOV/BCP/MENU-CREDIT.HTM

This site is the government's information site on credit and credit scams. Includes information on building better credit, divorce and credit, and credit insurance.

The 3 Credit Bureaus:

WWW.EXPERIAN.COM

This site includes credit education and how to get your credit report or credit score from Experian.

WWW.EQUIFAX.COM

This site offers identity theft insurance, credit watch services, and your credit report and score for a fee.

WWW.TRANSUNION.COM

This site claims to offer a 3-1 credit report plus free credit score. Also includes a consumer learning center.

CHAPTER 11

WHAT IS YOUR CREDIT SCORE & HOW IS IT DETERMINED

A credit score (also called a FICO score) is a specific number rating that helps lenders/creditors to determine how likely a person will be to repay their debts, based on their past credit history. The FICO score formula was created by Fair Isaac, and is used broadly by banks and creditors for the purpose of making decisions about creditors.

FICO scores range from 300 to 850, with a higher score being the more desirable score, and representing a lower credit risk. These scores can fluctuate from month to month, depending on a variety of a consumer's actions.

The FICO score's formula, as created by Fair Isaac, takes into consideration more than twenty factors in five different categories.

Approximately 35% of the score is based on how you pay your bills including recent payment activity, have you paid all of your bills on time, are all or some of your bills paid late, do you or have you had accounts in collection, and have you had a bankruptcy.

Another 30% or so of the equation by Fair Isaac looks at how much debt you owe, and what is available to you. This takes into consideration your credit cards, auto loans, mortgages, lines of credit, etc. Those who carry a lot of credit and use much or most of it present a credit risk. Also, those who carry a lot of available credit at any given time have the opportunity to use their available credit and may appear as a less attractive risk. People who consistently have their credit cards maxed out to the limit are also riskier, as they come across a situation where they may not be able to pay back their debt. The people with the best credit have credit available to them, but do not carry a balance from month to month.

Approximately 15% of the equation takes into consideration how long your credit history is. How long have you had credit with the same creditor? The longer your history is with the same creditor, the more points you will receive.

The remaining 20% of the formula reviews: whether or not you have a good balance of different types of credit; and how many new credit inquiries are on your credit report. When a consumer applies for several different loans or credit cards at the same time, their credit score will drop as a result. People who file for bankruptcy often spend as much as they can prior to filing.

Potential Reasons for a Poor FICO Score or Poor Credit History

Following (as taken from the Fair Isaac model) are a list of the potential reasons that your credit score may be lower than the highly desirable "perfect score of 850." These are some of the reasons that are used by Fair Isaac in their FICO credit score determination. A trained eye will recognize that it is not desirable to have too many or too little

accounts, too high or too low available credit lines, too new or too many

inquiries, and definitely no delinquencies, collections, public records, or

bankruptcy. The key is to recognize the factors that are considered by Fair

Isaac, and to know how your actions will affect these criteria.

- Amount owed on accounts is too high
- Level of delinquency on account
- Too few bank revolving accounts
- Proportion of loan balances to loan amounts is too high
- Too many bank or national revolving accounts
- Lack of recent installment loan information
- Too many accounts with balances
- Too many consumer finance company accounts
- Account payment history is too new to rate
- Too many inquiries within last 12 months
- Too many accounts recently opened
- Proportion of balances to credit limits is too high on bank revolving or other revolving accounts
- Amount owed on revolving accounts is too high
- Length of time revolving accounts have been established
- Time since delinquency is too recent or unknown
- Length of time accounts have been established
- Lack of recent bank revolving information
- Lack of recent revolving account information
- No recent non-mortgage balance information
- Number of accounts with delinquency
- Too few accounts currently paid as agreed
- Date of last inquiry too recent

- Length of time since derogatory public record or collection is too short
- Amount past due on accounts
- Serious delinquency, derogatory public record, or collection filed
- Number of bank or national revolving accounts with balances
- No recent revolving balances
- Length of time installment loans have been established
- Number of bank revolving or other revolving accounts
- Number of retail accounts
- Too few accounts currently paid as agreed
- Number of established accounts
- No recent bank card balances
- Date of last inquiry too recent
- Time since most recent account opening is too short
- Too few accounts with recent payment information
- Amount owed on delinquent accounts
- Lack of recent installment loan information
- Proportion of loan balances to loan amounts is too high
- Payments due on accounts
- Length of time open installment loans have been established
- Number of consumer finance company accounts established relative to length of consumer finance history
- Serious delinquency, and public record or collection filed
- Serious delinquency
- Derogatory public record or collection filed
- Number of consumer finance company inquiries
- Lack of recent auto loan information
- Length of time consumer finance company loans have been established
- Lack of recent consumer finance company account information
- Lack of recent mortgage loan information
- Proportion of balances to loan amounts on mortgage loans is too high
- Too few accounts with balances

- Number of consumer finance company inquiries
- Lack of recent retail account information
- Amount owed on retail accounts

CHAPTER 12

INTERESTING FACTS & THOUGHTS ABOUT CREDIT

While it can take a long time to fix credit mistakes, it only takes a short time or inattention, to hurt your credit score. Your credit history should be known, monitored, and you should think about how each and every financial decision can and will affect your credit history. This includes holiday purchases, vacation charges, as well as everyday needs.

Young adults should think about this at an early age. Creditors will deny an individual with no credit history. Also, if you have a relatively short history, and the one you have is poor, that will look even worse. Good habits need to start early. Know how your decisions will affect your future.

I have heard many young people say…"it doesn't matter, because I already have my car and don't plan on buying a house for a long time." I have also heard current homeowners say "I already own my home and own a car…what do I need to worry so much for?" Imagine that your employment situation changes and you need to move, purchase a new home, or make repairs to your existing home. Will you be able to take care of your basic housing needs, qualify for a mortgage, and replace that broken furnace?

Perhaps you haven't thought about the fact that your credit history will also affect the person you choose to marry one day, or the person you have already married.

If you have not made wise decisions in the past, change your actions now.

Credit Facts

- Your credit report may include personal information, employment information, loan and credit card payments including any delinquencies, amount of credit used vs. available, overdrawn bank account information, inquiries from creditors who you have authorized to check your credit, collection activity, late payments reported by utility companies, late child support payments, and any public record information.

- A credit score (also called a FICO score) is a number that helps lenders/creditors to determine how likely a person will be to repay their debts, based on their past credit history.

- FICO scores range from 300 to 850, with a higher score being the more desirable score, and representing a lower credit risk.

- FICO scores can fluctuate from month to month.

- Opening new credit accounts can actually lower your credit score.

- If a business or creditor account does not appear on your credit report, your history with that creditor will not affect your credit score (until that information is reported.)

- More than 25% of the people in the United States have delinquent information on their credit file.

- Moving your debt around (i.e. to a credit account that charges lower interest) will not necessarily improve your credit score. While it may save you interest charges, your credit report will show that you have more accounts, albeit the same debt, and your credit score may decrease. Interest rates are not reported to credit reporting agencies.

- Studies have shown a direct correlation between your financial history and your potential to file an insurance claim. Accordingly, insurance companies in most states are permitted to use your credit score in determining insurance premiums.

- While you believe that your credit is "private," it actually is very public, and can be viewed by new employers, mortgage companies, insurance companies, creditors, anyone that you authorize, and others.

- Thieves can go through your garbage and mail in hopes of stealing personal information to use to use your identity, open new accounts, redirect your mail, open a bank account in your name, and potentially avoid paying any debts they have established in your name.

- 50% of identity theft complaints made to the Federal Trade Commission are reported to be credit card accounts that were opened and used by another individual in the complainant's name.

- The way to improve your credit is to pay off outstanding debt, and make payments on time.

- Carrying a balance that is higher than 50% of your available credit can harm your credit. It is best to have in use 25% or less of your credit line at any time.

- Besides making on-time payments, good credit results from having a balanced number of types of credit (i.e. mortgage, auto loan, and maximum of 4-6 credit cards with balance of less than 50% of credit line in use.)

- If you arrange to "charge-off" your debts (agree to pay smaller amount and unpaid balance owed is "charged-off") this will adversely affect your credit and remain on your report for up to 7 years.

- If you make arrangements with a collection agency to pay less than the total owed amount, your credit report will indicate "paid for less than the total due."

- If you work with a debt management company, and payments are submitted by that agency, your debtor will report that your account is "Managed by Credit Counseling Company." This may appear as if you cannot handle your financial accounts in a responsible way yourself.

- You have the right to remove inaccurate or untimely information from your credit report.

- If you sign up for a pre-approved credit card, the bank will still run a credit check once you return the offer. This will show up as an inquiry on your credit report. If your credit report has new negative information, they may not offer you that "super low" promotional interest rate.

Your Credit Rights

If you have been denied credit for any reason, you have a right to be told what information in your credit file was used against you. Following a denial, a creditor will send you a letter detailing the reason(s) your request for credit was denied.

The creditor has a responsibility to let you know which credit reporting agency provided negative information about you, and what their negative reasons were.

Under your Fair Credit Reporting Rights, you will then have 60 days to request a free copy of the credit report that affected your creditor's decision. Once you receive the report, any derogatory information will be listed first as potentially negative information. Your report will also list everyone who has recently requested your credit report.

If there is inaccurate information in the credit report, you have the right to dispute that information. The credit-reporting agency that provided the report must investigate your dispute and provide you with a written report of its findings. In its investigation, the credit-reporting agency will notify your creditor of your dispute, and request that they commence a timely investigation of the facts. The creditor must then report its findings to the credit-reporting agency, and this must be completed within 30 days from the date the dispute was originally filed.

If the credit reporting agency receives its report from the creditor, and cannot resolve your complaint, you may request and issue a statement to be added to your credit report. Anyone who has recently requested your report can be notified of the investigation and of your statement.

Following your dispute and the credit reporting agency's investigation, any inaccurate information must be corrected or deleted within 30 days. Also, any negative information that is older than seven years must be removed from your report.

Accurate information will remain on your credit report for seven years.

Any Bankruptcy information must be removed from your credit report after 10 years (and sometimes after 7 years, depending on how you filed.)

Anyone who requests your credit report must have a permissible purpose under the FCRA. Permissible uses include: when ordered by a court, when approved in writing by a consumer, for the granting of credit as a result of an application or for collection purposes for that account, for employment (only when expressly consented by the consumer in writing), for insurance applications when consented by the consumer, when a creditor wants to determine whether a consumer meets the terms of their credit agreement, for determination of child support payments or enforcement, for the use of an investor or insurer to assess credit risks from an existing obligation, or as a result of a government application for licensing or to consider financial responsibility.

Any party who requests your credit report must make certification to the credit reporting agency that they are using the report for one of the above permissible uses.

Information may not be provided to your employer, landlord, or any other person without your written permission. Generally, when you fill out an application for credit, you must sign your consent to for the creditor to obtain your credit report. Once a creditor has granted you with credit, the fine print in your agreement with them gives them the right to periodically check your credit.

If a credit reporting agency violates any of these rights, you may bring legal action against them, citing a violation of your Fair Credit Reporting Rights.

Under the FCRA (see Chapter 7), you also have rights that protect you from having false information provided to a credit-reporting agency. Creditors may not knowingly provide false information. If false information is provided, the creditor must notify the credit-reporting agency of the correct information. If you notify a creditor that information they provided to the credit reporting agency is false, and it is proven to be false, the creditor must then notify the credit-reporting agency of the correct information.

Low-Rate Credit Card Offers

Credit card companies bombard you with credit card offers full of perks. Did you know that zero percent or low interest rate credit card you just sent for can cause your credit score to drop?

You should be aware that each credit card you open has an affect on your credit score. It is incorrect to assume that the more credit card/lines of credit you have, the better your credit will be. Each time you establish new lines of credit, each of your credit lines will remain on your credit report, whether you carry a balance or not. To a creditor, this means that at any time you can access that credit line and overspend or max it out.

Some credit cards promise low rates that are only "introductory rates." Read all of the fine print before signing for your new "low interest" credit card. Perhaps that low interest rate will really turn into a high interest rate. Also, if you fail to make a payment on time, your creditor may, under the terms of your Agreement, be able to raise your interest rate to something other than what you bargained for.

The best way to handle multiple credit card offers is to evaluate what your needs are, and research the best credit card interest rates. Watch out for those introductory rates. Look at the credit cards that don't charge an annual fee. Many credit cards also offer other programs for its members, such as membership rewards, frequent flier programs, or cash back based on your spending.

Debt Management Agencies/Advisors

If you are having trouble or cannot pay your debts, there are alternatives out there for you.

Most individuals cannot get through a program on cable television without hearing or seeing information about consolidating debt, lowering your interest rates, and paying off your debt fast and easy.

Many states do not regulate debt management agencies, and consumers should exercise care prior to signing up for this service. This is not to say that one of these agencies cannot help you, as a consumer.

Many debt management agencies charge an upfront fee for their services, and may also charge you a monthly fee as part of their program.

Some agencies are currently being investigated for failing to make payments to their clients' creditors, as promised and those clients end up with a worse credit report than prior to hiring an outside agency.

Prior to making any decision about enlisting the help of a Debt Management Agency, check out the company with your local Better Business Bureau, as well as in the state they are located in. Do not make any quick decisions, and read any contracts in their entirety prior to signing anything.

Also when considering your options, keep in mind that bankruptcy is a better option for most people. Your credit will be much better after bankruptcy than after you pay off your debts, and bankruptcy costs less.

Charge-Offs

A creditor can declare a debt as a "charge-off" if the creditor believes that they will be unable to collect a debt from a consumer. Generally this will happen when a consumer is seriously delinquent, and has not made any payment for many months. The debt is then written off by the creditor as "uncollectable." This is not an advisable solution to your financial difficulties.

When a charge-off occurs, a consumer remains responsible for the debt. The creditor may attempt to collect the debt through the use of a collection agency. There also remains the possibility that the consumer can be sued by the creditor to collect the outstanding debt.

When a consumer has a charge-off on their credit report, this is one of the most negative items that can appear on a credit report. This item will remain on a consumer's credit report for up to 7 years, commencing from the date of original delinquency. Other creditors will view this item as a debt that a consumer incurred, but failed to pay off.

Once an item has been listed as a charge-off on a credit report, payment of the outstanding debt will not remove the information from a consumer's credit report. Instead, the classification will be changed to read "Paid Charge-Off."

A consumer may also negotiate with a creditor to pay off an account, for an amount that is less than the full amount due. The remainder of the amount due is a charge-off to a creditor. A creditor is under no obligation to accept a smaller amount for full satisfaction of the debt; this is totally their discretion. If attempting to negotiate a smaller amount as full satisfaction of a debt, a consumer must retain all paperwork and request every promise from the creditor in writing. Creditors may agree to keep from reporting this information to a credit-reporting agency, but any guarantee of this should be issued in writing and retained by the consumer.

Bankruptcy

While filing for bankruptcy is becoming increasingly more popular (in 2003, more than 1.6 million people in the United States filed for bankruptcy), it should be considered only as a last alternative to resolving financial difficulties. Bankruptcy is a legal filing wherein a consumer publicly and legally declares that they are unable to pay their debts. The bankruptcy filing will remain on your credit report for 7-10 years.

When a consumer files for Chapter 7 bankruptcy, the consumer is responsible for turning various properties over to a trustee who sells the debtor's property to pay his or her debts off.

With a Chapter 13 bankruptcy filing, a debtor's income and assets are reviewed to determine a fair payment plan that the court will approve, and which the debtor will be able to make payments. Often, the debtor is able to keep their home or car if they choose this type of filing. Under this type of filing, any attempts by a mortgage company or auto lender to repossess the home or automobile are suspended pending establishment of a payment plan.

It is always best to consult with an attorney prior to making any decisions regarding bankruptcy, to be sure you have exhausted all of your other alternatives, and that you are making the right choice for you.

Following a bankruptcy, it will be difficult to be granted credit, and a consumer will be most likely be granted "sub-prime" offers (meaning they will pay a much higher interest rate.) Prior to making this decision, you should be at the point where you have not made payments and are unable to make your payments or repay your debt.

Protecting Your Credit During and After Divorce

When facing a divorce, one of the important considerations should be to protect your credit history.

If it is a friendly divorce, an agreement should be reached as to who will be responsible for which debt. Otherwise, an attorney can assist with this process. Prior to hiring the attorney, payments should continue to be made. Prior to the finalization of any divorce, these responsibilities should be made, in writing, and included with the divorce.

This process can commence by closing any joint accounts to eliminate further charges. This involves either a telephone call or letter in writing to a creditor requesting that the account be closed permanently. Of course, the balances will also need to be paid. Continue to make the payments on any debts that are in your name alone, and make arrangements as to who should be paying each debt on joint accounts. In the meantime, all payments must be made on time by one or both of the parties to protect the integrity of the credit histories. In the event one or both of the parties stop paying for a debt that is in both parties' names, the delinquency will show up on both credit reports.

The next step should be to notify the creditors and credit reporting agencies of the divorce. You should also provide any other pertinent information, such as address changes.

This is a very important time to monitor your credit report. Any discrepancies in your agreement with your spouse should be taken care of immediately. You should notify your attorney if your former spouse has caused a delinquency on your report for a bill that he or she is to be responsible for. Also, watch for any new accounts being opened in your name that you are unaware of.

When a Spouse Dies

If your spouse passes away, suddenly or otherwise, this is a time that your credit report should be carefully reviewed.

There have been many instances wherein a spouse obtained credit and or debt that the other spouse had no idea of. Even if that is not the case, it is important to make an assessment of what your monthly obligations will be from now on.

When reviewing the credit report, determine which bills are listed in your name, which were jointly held, and which were solely in your spouse's name. You should continue to make any payments for accounts that are held jointly in your name with your spouse, and those accounts that you are responsible for solely.

Prior to continuing to pay on a debt that was held solely by your spouse, you should consult with an experienced estate attorney. We are not suggesting in any way that you stop paying these bills. We are merely suggesting that perhaps there are some debts that are owed by your late spouse's estate, and not you personally.

Depending on what state you live in, you may still be responsible for paying these debts. There are, however, some states wherein you would not be responsible for repayment of a debt that was solely in your spouse's name. His or her estate would be responsible for any of those debts. A competent estate attorney can advise you regarding which bills you should be responsible for paying.

Contact your creditors and notify them of your spouse's death. You may also wish to close all joint accounts at that time (close off to any further charging.) Your creditor can discuss opening a new account solely in your name at that time, if you need them. Remember, it is good to continue to establish your own credit history, specifically if your spouse handled all of your financial affairs and you have little or no credit history.

If the accounts were held solely by your late spouse, you may wish to have the creditor send you a letter in writing that the account will be closed, they will not be holding you responsible (as you never signed for that particular account), and that they should file a claim against your late spouse's estate for any outstanding balance. Of course, you should also review this with your spouse's estate attorney and obtain their legal advice.

When meeting with your attorney, bring along a copy of your credit report, as well as a list of any other assets or debts held by you or your spouse, and copies of deed's or title paperwork.

CHAPTER 13

STATE-BY-STATE RESOURCES
(Attorney General, Consumer Protection
Agencies, Banking Authority)

If you believe that your rights have been violated with regard to the provisions of the Fair Credit Reporting Act, consider contacting your local Attorney General to commence an investigation.

Attorney General (By State)

Alabama: Troy King   (334) 242-7300
              State House
              11 S. Union St.
              Montgomery, AL 36130
              http://www.ago.state.al.us

Alaska: Gregg Renkes   (907) 465-3600
              P.O.Box 110300
              Diamond Courthouse
              Juneau, AK 99811-0300
              http://www.law.state.ak.us

American: *Samoa*	Fiti Sunia P.O.Box 7 Pago Pago, AS 96799 http://www.samoanet.com	(684) 633-4163
Arizona:	Terry Goddard 1275 W. Washington St. Phoenix, AZ 85007 http://www.attorneygeneral.state.az.us	(602) 542-5025
Arkansas:	Mike Beebe 200 Tower Bldg. 323 Center St. Little Rock, AR 72201-2610 http://www.ag.state.ar.us	(800) 482-8982
California:	Bill Lockyer 1300 I St., Ste. 1740 Sacramento, CA 95814 http://caag.state.ca.us	(916) 445-9555

Colorado:	Ken Salazar Dept. of Law 1525 Sherman St. Denver, CO 80203 http://www.ago.state.co.us	(303) 866-4500
Connecticut:	Richard Blumenthal 55 Elm St. Hartford, CT 06141-0120 http://www.cslib.org/attygenl/	(860) 808-5318
Delaware:	M. Jane Brady Carvel State Office Bldg. 820 N. French St. Wilmington, DE 19801 http://www.state.de.us/attgen	(302) 577-8400
District of: *Columbia*	Robert J. Spagnoletti Office of the Corporation Counsel 441 4th St., NW, Washington, DC 20001 http://occ.dc.gov	(202) 724-1305

Florida:	Charlie Crist	(850) 245-0140
	The Capitol	
	PL 01	
	Tallahassee, FL 32399-1050	
	http://myfloridalegal.com/	

Georgia:	Thurbert E. Baker	(404) 656-3300
	40 Capitol Square, SW	
	Atlanta, GA 30334-1300	
	http://ganet.org/ago/	

Guam:	Douglas Moylan	(671) 475-3409
	Judicial Center Bldg.	
	Ste. 2-200E,	
	120 W. O'Brien Dr.	
	Hagatna, Guam 96910	
	http://www.guamattorneygeneral.com/	

Hawaii:	Mark J. Bennett	(808) 586-1500
	425 Queen St.	
	Honolulu, HI 96813	
	http://www.state.hi.us/ag/index.html	

Idaho:	Lawrence Wasden	(208) 334-2400
	Statehouse	
	Boise, ID 83720-1000	
	http://www2.state.id.us/ag/	

Illinois:	Lisa Madigan	(312) 814-3000
	James R. Thompson Ctr.	
	100 W. Randolph St.	
	Chicago, IL 60601	
	http://www.ag.state.il.us	

Indiana:	Steve Carter	(317) 232-6201
	Indiana Government Center South	
	5th Floor	
	302 West Washington Street	
	Indianapolis, IN 46204	
	http://www.in.gov/attorneygeneral/	

Iowa:	Tom Miller	(515) 281-5164
	Hoover State Office Bldg.	
	1305 E. Walnut	
	Des Moines, IA 50319	
	http://www.IowaAttorneyGeneral.org	

Kansas:	Phill Kline	(785) 296-2215
	120 S.W. 10th Ave.	
	2nd Floor	
	Topeka, KS 66612-1597	
	http://www.ink.org/public/ksag	

Kentucky:	Gregory D. Stumbo	(502) 696-5300
	State Capitol	
	Suite 118	
	Frankfort, KY 40601	
	http://www.law.state.ky.us	

Louisiana:	Charles C. Foti, Jr	(225) 326-6000
	Dept. of Justice	
	P.O.Box 94095	
	Baton Rouge, LA 70804-9095	
	http://www.ag.state.la.us/	

Maine:	G. Steven Rowe	(207) 626-8800
	State House Station 6	
	Augusta, ME 04333	
	http://www.state.me.us/ag	

Maryland:	J. Joseph Curran Jr.	(410) 576-6300
	200 St. Paul Place	
	Baltimore, MD 21202-2202	
	http://www.oag.state.md.us	

Massachusetts:	Tom Reilly	(617) 727-2200
	1 Ashburton Place	
	Boston, MA 02108-1698	
	http://www.ago.state.ma.us	

Michigan:	Mike Cox	(517) 373-1110
	P.O.Box 30212	
	525 W. Ottawa St.	
	Lansing, MI 48909-0212	
	http://www.ag.state.mi.us	

Minnesota:	Mike Hatch	(800) 657-3787
	State Capitol, Ste. 102,	
	St. Paul, MN 55155	
	http://www.ag.state.mn.us	

Mississippi:	Jim Hood	(601) 359-3680
	Dept. of Justice	
	P.O.Box 220	
	Jackson, MS 39205-0220	
	http://www.ago.state.ms.us	

Missouri:	Jeremiah W. Nixon	(573) 751-3321
	Supreme Ct. Bldg.	
	207 W. High St.	
	Jefferson City, MO 65101	
	http://www.ago.state.mo.us	

Montana:	Mike McGrath	(406) 444-2026
	Justice Building,	
	215 N. Sanders	
	Helena, MT 59620-1401	
	http://doj.state.mt.us/	

Nebraska:	Jon Bruning	(402) 471-2682
	2115 State Capitol	
	P.O.Box 98920	
	Lincoln, NE 68509-8920	
	http://www.ago.state.ne.us	

Nevada: Brian Sandoval   (775) 684-1100
                     100 N. Carson St.
                     Carson City, NV 89701
                     http://ag.state.nv.us/

New Hampshire: Peter Heed   (603) 271-3658
                     33 Capitol Street
                     Concord, NH 03301-6397
                     http://www.state.nh.us/nhdoj

New Jersey: Peter C. Harvey   (609) 292-8740
                     Richard J. Hughes Justice Complex
                     25 Market St.
                     PO Box 080
                     Trenton, NJ 08625
                     http://www.state.nj.us/lps/

New Mexico: Patricia A. Madrid   (505) 827-6000
                     P.O. Drawer 1508
                     Sante Fe, NM 87504-1508
                     http://www.ago.state.nm.us

New York:	Eliot Spitzer	(518) 474-7330
	Dept. of Law - The Capitol	
	2nd fl.	
	Albany, NY 12224	
	http://www.oag.state.ny.us	

North Carolina:	Roy Cooper	(919) 716-6400
	Dept. of Justice	
	P.O.Box 629	
	Raleigh, NC 27602-0629	
	http://www.jus.state.nc.us	

North Dakota:	Wayne Stenehjem	(701) 328-2210
	State Capitol	
	600 E. Boulevard Ave.	
	Bismarck, ND 58505-0040	
	http://www.ag.state.nd.us	

Northern:	Pamela Brown	(670) 664-2341
Mariana	2nd Floor	
Islands	Honorable Juan A. Sablan Memorial Bldg.	
	Capitol Hill,	
	Saipan, MP 96950	

Ohio:	Jim Petro	(614) 466-4320
	State Office Tower	
	30 E. Broad St.	
	Columbus, OH 43215-3428	
	http://www.ag.state.oh.us	
Oklahoma:	W. A. Drew Edmondson	(405) 521-3921
	State Capitol	
	Rm. 112	
	2300 N. Lincoln Blvd.	
	Oklahoma City, OK 73105	
	http://www.oag.state.ok.us	
Oregon:	Hardy Myers	(503) 378-4400
	Justice Building	
	1162 Court Street	
	NE, Salem, OR 97301-4096	
	http://www.doj.state.or.us	
Pennsylvania:	Gerald J. Pappert	(717) 787-3391
	1600 Strawberry Square	
	Harrisburg, PA 17120	
	http://www.attorneygeneral.gov	

Puerto Rico: Anabelle Rodriguez   (787) 721 7700
P.O.Box 9020192
San Juan, PR 00902-0192
http://www.justicia.gobierno.pr

Rhode Island: Patrick Lynch   (401) 274-4400
150 S. Main St.
Providence, RI 02903
http://www.riag.state.ri.us

South Carolina: Henry McMaster   (803) 734-3970
Rembert C. Dennis Office Bldg.
P.O.Box 11549
Columbia, SC 29211-1549
http://www.scattorneygeneral.org

South Dakota: Larry Long   (605) 773-3215
500 E. Capitol
Pierre, SD 57501-5070
www.state.sd.us/attorney/attorney.html

Tennessee:	Paul G. Summers 500 Charlotte Ave. Nashville, TN 37243 http://www.attorneygeneral.state.tn.us	(615) 741-5860
Texas:	Greg Abbott Capitol Station P.O.Box 12548 Austin, TX 78711-2548 http://www.oag.state.tx.us	(512) 463-2100
Utah:	Mark Shurtleff PO Box 142320, Salt Lake City, UT 84114-2320 http://attorneygeneral.utah.gov/	(801) 538-9600
Vermont:	William H. Sorrell 109 State St. Montpelier, VT 05609-1001 http://www.state.vt.us/atg	(802) 828-3173

Virginia:	Jerry Kilgore	(804) 786-2071

Virginia: Jerry Kilgore (804) 786-2071
900 E. Main St.
Richmond, VA 23219
http://www.oag.state.va.us

Virgin Islands: Iver A. Stridiron (D) (340) 774-5666
Dept. of Justice
G.E.R.S. Complex 48B-50C Kronprinsdens
Gade, St. Thomas, VI 00802

Washington: Christine O. Gregoire (360) 753-6200
P.O.Box 40100
1125 Washington St., SE,
Olympia, WA 98504-0100
http://www.atg.wa.gov/

West Virginia: Darrell Vivian McGraw Jr. (304) 558-2021
State Capitol
1900 Kanawha Blvd. E.,
Charleston, WV 25305
http://www.wvs.state.wv.us/wvag

Wisconsin:	Peg Lautenschlager	(608) 266-1221
	114 East - State Capitol	
	Madison, WI 53702	
	http://www.doj.state.wi.us	

Wyoming:	Pat Crank	(307) 777-7841
	123 State Capitol Bldg.	
	Cheyenne, WY 82002	
	http://attorneygeneral.state.wy.us	

Credit Reporting Agencies:

The 3 major credit reporting agencies are:

Equifax 1-800-685-1111 www.equifax.com

Experian 1-888-397-3742 www.experian.com

Trans Union 1-800-916-8800 www.transunion.com

Consumer Protection

If you have a complaint about a credit reporting agency, make your complaint to the following Federal agency:

Federal Trade Commission   www.ftc.gov
Consumer Response Center – FCRA
Washington, DC 20580
202-326-3761

Banking Authority (By State)

Alabama   Superintendent of Banks
Center for Commerce
401 Adams Ave., #680
Montgomery, AL 36130-1201
334-242-3452
Fax: 334-242-3500
Web site: www.legislature.state.al.us

Alaska   Director of Banking
Division of Banking Securities and Corporations
Department of Commerce
150 Third St., Room 217
Juneau, AK 99811-0807
907-465-2521
TDD: 907-465-5437
Fax: 907-465-2549
Web site: www.dced.state.ak.us/bsc/bsc.htm

Arizona   Superintendent of Banks
Arizona State Banking Department
2910 North 44th St.
Suite 310
Phoenix, AZ 85018

602-255-4421
Toll free in AZ: 1-800-544-0708
Fax: 602-381-1225
Web site: www.azbanking.com

Arkansas   Arkansas State Bank Department
400 Hardin Rd.
Suite 100
Little Rock, AR 72201
501-324-9019
Fax: 501-324-9028
Web site: www.accessarkansas.org/bank

California   Commissioner
Department of Financial Institutions
State of California
111 Pine St., Suite 1100
San Francisco, CA 94111
415-263-8507
Toll free in CA: 1-800-622-0620
Fax: 415-989-5310
Web site: www.dfi.ca.gov

Colorado	State Bank Commissioner
	Department of Regulatory Agencies
	Division of Banking
	1560 Broadway
	Suite 1175
	Denver, CO 80202
	303-894-7575
	Fax: 303-894-7570
	E-mail: banking@dora.state.co.us
	Web site: www.dora.state.co.us/banking/

Connecticut	Banking Commissioner
	Connecticut Department of Banking
	260 Constitution Plaza
	Hartford, CT 06103
	860-240-8200
	Toll free in CT: 1-800-831-7225
	Fax: 860-240-8178
	Web site: www.state.ct.us/dob

Delaware	State Bank Commissioner
	Office of the State Bank Commissioner
	555 East Lockerman St., Suite 210
	Dover, DE 19901
	302-739-4235
	Fax: 302-739-3609
	Web site: www.state.de.us/bank

District of Columbia	Commissioner of Banking and Financial Institutions Department of Banking & Financial Institutions 1400 L St., NW Washington, DC 20005 202-727-1563 Fax: 202-727-1290 Web site: www.dbfi.dc.gov
Florida	Department of Financial Services 200 East Gaines St. Tallahassee, FL 323990300 850-413-3100 Toll free in FL: 1-800-342-2762 TDD toll free: 1-800-640-0886 Fax: 850-488-2349 Web site: www.fldfs.com
Georgia	Legal & Consumer Affairs Specialist State of Georgia Dept of Banking & Finance 2990 Brandywine Rd., Suite 200 Atlanta, GA 30341-5565 770-986-1653 770-986-1633 Fax: 770-986-1657 Web site: www.gadbf.org

Hawaii   Commissioner
State of Hawaii Department of Commerce
& Consumer Affairs
Financial Institutions
1010 Richards St., Room 602A
Honolulu, HI 96805
808-586-2820
Toll free in Kauai: 1-800-274-3141
Toll free in Maui: 1-800-984-2400
Toll free in Hawaii: 1-800-974-4000
808-586-2820
Fax: 808-586-2818

Idaho   Director
Idaho Department of Finance
PO Box 83720
Boise, ID 83720-0031
208-332-8000
Toll free in ID: 1-888-346-3376
Fax: 208-332-8098
E-mail: finance@fin.state.id.us
Web site: finance.state.id.us

Illinois	Commissioner of Banks and Real Estate Office of Banks and Real Estate 310 South Michigan Ave., Suite 2130 Chicago, IL 60604 312-793-3000 Toll free: 1-877-793-3470 TDD: 312-793-0291 Fax: 312-793-7097
Indiana	Department of Financial Institutions 402 West Washington St. Room W-066 Indianapolis, IN 46204-2759 317-232-3955 Toll free in IN: 1-800-382-4880 Fax: 317-232-7655 Web site: www.dfi.state.in.us
Iowa	Superintendent of Banking Iowa Division of Banking 200 East Grand, Suite 300 Des Moines, IA 503091827 515-281-4014 Toll free nationwide: 1-800-972-2018 Fax: 515-281-4862 Web site: www.idob.state.ia.us

Kansas	State Bank Commissioner Office of the State Bank Commissioner 700 Jackson St., Suite 300 Topeka, KS 66603-3714 785-296-2266 Fax: 785-296-0168 Web site: www.osbckansas.org
Kentucky	Commissioner Department of Financial Institutions 1025 Capitol Center Dr. Suite 200 Frankfort, KY 40601 502-573-3390 Toll free: 1-800-223-2579 Fax: 502-573-8787 Web site: www.dfi.state.ky.us
Louisiana	Acting Commissioner LA Office of Financial Institutions PO Box 94095 Baton Rouge, LA 70804-9095 225-925-4660 Fax: 225-925-4524 E-mail: la_ofi@mail.premier.net Web site: www.ofi.state.la.us

Maine	Superintendent of Banking Maine Bureau of Financial Institions 36 State House Station Augusta, ME 04333-0036 207-624-8570 Toll free: 1-800-965-5235 TDD: 207-624-8563 Fax: 207-624-8590 Web site: www.mainebankingreg.org
Maryland	Commissioner of Financial Regulation Division 500 North Calvert St. Baltimore, MD 21202 410-333-6808 Toll free in MD: 1-888-784-0136 Fax: 410-333-0475 Web site: www.dllr.state.md.us/finance/
Massachusetts	Commissioner of Banks Massachusetts Division of Banks One South Station Boston, MA 02110 617-956-1500 Toll free in MA: 1-800-495-2265 TDD: 617-956-1577 Fax: 617-956-1597 Web site: www.mass.gov/dob

Michigan	Commissioner Office of Financial and Insurance Services Office of the Commissioner 611 W. Ottawa St., 2nd Floor Lansing, MI 48933 517-373-3460 Fax: 517-335-4978 Web site: www.cis.state.mi.us/ofis
Minnesota	Deputy Commissioner Minnesota Department of Commerce Financial Examinations Division 85 Seventh Place East, Suite 500 St. Paul, MN 55101 651-296-2715 Fax: 651-296-8591 Web site: www.state.mn.us/
Mississippi	Director Consumer Finance Division Department of Banking and Consumer Finance Consumer Finance PO Box 23729 Jackson, MS 39205-3729 601-359-1031 Toll free in MS: 1-800-844-2499 Fax: 601-359-3557 Web site: www.dbcf.state.ms.us

Missouri	Acting Commissioner of Finance
	Department of Finance
	PO Box 716
	Jefferson City, MO 65102
	573-751-3242
	Fax: 573-751-9192
	E-mail: finance@mail.state.mo.us
	Web site: www.missouri-finance.org
Montana	Commissioner
	Diivision of Banking & Financial Institutions
	301 South Park, Suite 316
	Helena, MT 59620-0546
	406-841-2920
	Fax: 406-841-2930
	www.discoveringmontana.com/doa/banking
Nebraska	Director
	Nebraska Department of Banking & Finance
	1200 N. St., Suite 311
	Lincoln, NE 68509
	402-471-2171
	Fax: 402-471-3062
	Web site: www.ndbf.org

Nevada Commissioner
Department of Business & Industry
Financial Institutions Division
406 East Second St., Suite 3
Carson City, NV 89701-4758
775-684-1830
Toll free in NV: 1-800-521-0019
Fax: 775-684-1845
Web site: www.fid.state.nv.us

New Hampshire State of New Hampshire Banking Department
Consumer Credit
64B Old Suncook Rd.
Concord, NH 03301
603-271-3561
TTY/TDD: 1-800-735-2964
Fax: 603-271-1090
Web site: www.state.nh.us/banking

New Jersey Acting Commissioner
Department of Banking and Insurance
20 West State St.
P.O. Box 325
Trenton, NJ 08625
609-292-3420 (banking)
Fax: 609-984-5273
Web site: www.state.nj.us/dobi/

New Mexico Financial Institutions Division
Regulation and Licensing Dept
725 St Michaels Drive
Santa Fe, NM 87501
505-827-7100
Fax: 505-827-7107
Web site: http://www.rld.state.nm.us/FID/

New York Superintendent of Banking
New York State Banking Department
Two Rector St.
New York, NY 10006-1894
212-618-6553
Toll free in NY: 1-800-522-3330
(consumer services hotline)
Toll free in NY: 1-800-832-1838
(small business information)
Fax: 212-618-6599
Web site: www.banking.state.ny.us

North Carolina NC Commissioner of Banks
North Carolina Commissioner of Banks
4309 Mail Service Center
Raleigh, NC 27699-4309
919-733-3016
Fax: 919-733-6918
Web site: www.banking.state.nc.us

North Dakota Commissioner
Department of Financial Institutions
2000 Schafer St.
Suite G
Bismarck, ND 58501-1204
701-328-9933
TDD toll free in ND: 1-800-366-6888
Fax: 701-328-9955
Web site: www.discovernd.com/dfi

Ohio   Training and Communications Manager
Department of Commerece - State of Ohio
Financial Institutions Division
77 South High St.
21st Floor
Columbus, OH 432156120
614-728-8400
Fax: 614-644-1631
Web site: www.com.state.oh.us/ODOC/dfi/

Oklahoma   Bank Commissioner
Oklahoma State Banking Department
4545 North Lincoln Blvd., Suite 164
Oklahoma City, OK 73105
405-521-2782
Fax: 405-522-2993
Web site: www.osbd.state.ok.us

Oregon	Administrator
	Department of Consumer & Business Services
	Division of Finance & Corporate
	350 Winter St., NE
	Room 410
	Salem, OR 97310
	503-378-4140
	Fax: 503-947-7862
	Web site: www.oregondfcs.org
Pennsylvania	Secretary of Banking Department
	The Pennsylvania Department of Banking
	333 Market St.
	16th Floor
	Harrisburg, PA 17101-2290
	717-787-6991
	Fax: 717-787-8773
	Web site: www.banking.state.pa.us
Puerto Rico	Commissioner
	Department of Financial Institutions
	Fernandez Juncos Station
	PO Box 11855
	San Juan, PR 00917-3855
	787-723-3131
	Fax: 787-723-4042
	Web site: www.cif.gov.pr

Rhode Island Associate Director and Superintendent
Division of Banking
Banking
233 Richmond St., Suite 231
Providence, RI 02903-4231
401-222-2405
401-222-2999
Fax: 401-222-5628

South Carolina Commissioner of Banking
State Board of Financial Institutions
1015 Sumter St.
Room 309
Columbia, SC 29201
803-734-2001
Fax: 803-734-2013

South Dakota Director
S.D. Division of Banking
217 1/2 W. Missouri Ave.
Pierre, SD 57501-4590
605-773-3421
Fax: 605-773-5367
Web site: www.state.sd.us/banking

Tennessee	Commissioner
	Tennessee Department of Financial Institutions
	The Nashville City Center
	511 Union Street, 4th Floor
	Nashville, TN 37219
	615-741-2236
	Fax: 615-741-2883
	E-mail: kayce.stoker@state.tn.us
	Web site: www.state.tn.us/financialinst/
Texas	Banking Commissioner
	Texas Department of Banking
	2601 North Lamar
	Austin, TX 78705
	512-475-1300
	Toll free in TX: 1-877-276-5554
	Fax: 512-475-1313
	Web site: www.banking.state.tx.us
Utah	Commissioner
	Department of Financial Institutions
	PO Box 146800
	Salt Lake City, UT 841146800
	801-538-8854
	Fax: 801-538-8894
	Web site: www.dfi.utah.gov

Vermont	Information Policy & Program Chief
	State of Vermont
	Banking, Insurance, Securities and Health Care
	89 Main St., Drawer 20
	Montpelier, VT 05620-3101
	802-828-4872
	Toll free: 1-800-964-1764
	Fax: 802-828-3306
	Web site: www.bishca.state.vt.us
Virgin Islands	Lieutenant Governor
	Commissioner of Insurance
	Chairman of Banking Board
	Kongen's Gade #18
	Charlotte Amalie
	St. Thomas, VI 00802
	340-774-2991
	Fax: 340-774-6953
Virginia	Commissioner
	Bureau of Financial Institutions
	1300 East Main St., Suite 800
	Richmond, VA 23218-0640
	804-371-9657
	Toll free in VA: 1-800-552-7945
	Fax: 804-371-9416
	Web site: www.state.va.us/scc

Washington   Director, Department of Financial Institutions
PO Box 41200
Olympia, WA 98504-1200
360-902-8707
Toll free: 1-800-372-8303
Fax: 360-586-5068
Web site: www.wa.gov/dfi

West Virginia Commissoner
State Capitol Complex
Division of Banking
Building 3, Room 311
1900 Kanawha Blvd. East
Charleston, WV 25305-0240
304-558-2294
Toll free in WV: 1-800-642-9056
Fax: 304-558-0442
Web site: www.wvdob.org

Wisconsin   Secretary
Department of Financial Institutions
345 West Washington Ave., 5th Floor
Madison, WI 53708-8861
608-267-1709
Toll free in WI: 1-800-452-3328
Fax: 608-264-7968
Web site: www.wdfi.org

Wyoming   Commissioner
Division of Banking
Herschler Bldg.
3rd Floor, East
Cheyenne, WY 82002
307-777-7797
Fax: 307-777-3555
E-mail: banking@state.wy.us
Web site: audit.state.wy.us/banking

CHAPTER 14

GLOSSARY/EXPLANATION OF TERMS

Annual Fee – An annual (yearly) charge to have and or keep a card or credit line. Some cards charge an annual fee, and others do not.

Annual Percentage Rate – The amount of interest a consumer will pay for credit on an annual basis.

Available Credit – The amount of credit available to you by a creditor. This figure takes into consideration your total credit line less any amounts that you owe for charges you have previously made.

Asset – Something that you own that has a money value, such as real estate, savings accounts, property, retirement accounts, etc.

Balance Transfer – The process of moving debt from one card or account to another. Generally individuals do this to switch their debt to a lower interest rate. There can be a fee associated with this. Banks often provide promotional rates to encourage consumers to transfer balances from another creditor to an account with their institution.

Bankruptcy – A legal filing wherein a consumer publicly and legally declares that they are unable to pay their debts. Bankruptcy will remain on an individual's credit report for 7-10 years. The Court will sell assets to cover the debts, or set up a debt repayment plan wherein a consumer may keep their property.

Charge-Off – When a consumer has not or does not repay for a debt, the creditor makes a "charge-off" wherein they write off that particular debt as un-collectable. This information will be reported to a consumer's credit report and will remain for 7 years.

Closing Date – The last day of your billing cycle. Any payments received following this date will be recorded on the next month's statement.

Collateral – Property offered to secure a credit account or loan. If the loan is not paid, a creditor may take back the property to partially or fully satisfy the debt.

Co-Signer – Another individual who legally agrees to be responsible for repayment of a debt, to assist another consumer with being approved for a loan. If the debtor fails to make their payments as agreed, the co-signer remains responsible for the debt, and their credit can and will be adversely affected if the payments are late or unpaid.

Credit – When a consumer wishes to defer payment of a debt, but promises to make payments with interest at a later date and possibly monthly. A creditor provides the "credit" in exchange for the debt being established, and the debtor agrees to pay over time.

Credit Card – A card provided by various creditors with which a consumer may make purchases, and has agreed in the original "credit card agreement" as to how the purchases and debt will be repaid, and at what interest rate.

Credit History – A history of how a consumer has borrowed, made payments, and how many accounts are open, closed, paid, in collection, and amounts of credit lines are available at any given time.

Creditor – A person or company that extends credit to a consumer, in exchange for a promise to pay at a later date with interest.

Due Date – The final date that a creditor must receive a payment of at least the minimum amount due on an account.

FICO – Fair Isaac Credit established a scoring system that uses statistical information, combined with a consumer's past credit history, to determine how likely that consumer will be to repay their debts. A number between 350 and 850 is assigned to each consumer by FICO. Creditors use this information to approve or deny credit to an individual.

Finance Charge – The actual amount of interest that is being charged to a consumer for any particular month. This amount often varies and is based on the annual percentage rate applied to an outstanding credit balance.

Minimum Monthly Payment – The smallest amount a consumer may pay for a particular month to remain in compliance with a creditor in accordance with the terms of their original credit agreement.

Posting Date – The date on which a payment is actually entered into a consumer's account by a creditor. This date may be later than the date the transaction was initially authorized by the consumer. This date should not be confused with the Transaction Date.

Secured Account – A credit card or account that is "secured" with property or cash. Often someone with poor credit can obtain a "secured credit card" wherein they prepay for the credit card, to reestablish their credit history.

Service Charge – Penalty amounts that are charged to a consumer by a creditor for extra items such as being over their limit, failing to make a minimum monthly payment, or any other items that have been included in the original Agreement between the two parties.

Statement – An accounting provided by a creditor to a consumer of the activity for a particular account in any given time-frame (often monthly or quarterly.) In many instances, the consumer must pay their debt to the creditor from the statement.

Statute of Limitations – A time limit imposed by a Federal or State government within which an individual may file a claim for something. The applicable Statute of Limitations varies by State (if a State matter) and by the subject matter.

Transaction Date – The date on which a consumer authorizes a transaction to occur, such as a charge or payment. This should not be confused with the Posting Date.

ABOUT THE PUBLISHER

ABOUT THE PUBLISHER

BOCA PRESS LLC

BOCA PRESS LLC fills the informational needs of individuals by publishing how-to and reference books.

BOCA PRESS LLC can be contacted at:

Information Director
Boca Press LLC
c/o Robin Shapiro
700 First Federal Plaza
Rochester, NY 14614
Fax (585) 262-6361

NOTES

Printed in the United States
24635LVS00003B/223-243

9 781883 527082